AUTOBIOGRAPHY

This volume provides a wide-ranging introduction to the study of autobiography.

In examining the historical tradition of the genre, Linda Anderson ranges across canonical and non-canonical texts and looks closely at twentieth-century women's writing, black and postcolonial writing. She explores the ideological assumptions about the nature of the self that underlie autobiographical writing, particularly in the light of recent feminist, psychoanalytic and poststructuralist criticism. As well as providing a comprehensive introduction to the forms and uses of the genre, this volume introduces the crucial questions of identity, selfhood, language and writing which lie at the heart of the related critical investigations.

This comprehensive and challenging guide is the ideal starting-point for all readers interested in autobiography.

Linda Anderson is Professor of Modern English and American Literature at the University of Newcastle upon Tyne. Her recent publications include *Women and Autobiography in the Twentieth Century* (1997), *Women's Lives/Women's Times* (edited with Trev Broughton, 1996) and *Territories of Desire in Queer Culture* (edited with David Alderson, 2000).

THE NEW CRITICAL IDIOM

SERIES EDITOR: JOHN DRAKAKIS, UNIVERSITY OF STIRLING

The New Critical Idiom is an invaluable series of introductory guides to today's critical terminology. Each book:

- provides a handy, explanatory guide to the use (and abuse) of the term
- offers an original and distinctive overview by a leading literary and cultural critic
- relates the term to the larger field of cultural representation.

With a strong emphasis on clarity, lively debate and the widest possible breadth of examples, *The New Critical Idiom* is an indispensable approach to key topics in literary studies.

Also available in this series:

AUTOBIOGRAPHY

Linda Anderson

LONDON AND NEW YORK

First published 2001 by Routledge
11 New Fetter Lane, London EC4P 4EE

Simultaneously published in the USA and Canada
by Routledge
29 West 35th Street, New York, NY 10001

Routledge is an imprint of the Taylor & Francis Group

© 2001 Linda Anderson

Typeset in Garamond by Keystroke, Jacaranda Lodge, Wolverhampton
Printed and bound in Great Britain by Clays Ltd, St Ives plc

British Library Cataloguing in Publication Data
A catalogue record for this book is available from the British Library

Library of Congress Cataloging in Publication Data
Anderson, Linda R., 1950–
Autobiography / Linda Anderson.
    p. cm. — (The new critical idiom)
    Includes bibliographical references and index.
    1. Autobiography. I. Title. II. Series.
    CT25 .A53 2001
    809'.93592—dc21   00–051704

ISBN 0–415–18634–X (hbk)
ISBN 0–415–18635–8 (pbk)

For Ann

CONTENTS

SERIES EDITOR'S PREFACE

The New Critical Idiom is a series of introductory books which seeks to extend the lexicon of literary terms, in order to address the radical changes which have taken place in the study of literature during the last decades of the twentieth century. The aim is to provide clear, well-illustrated accounts of the full range of terminology currently in use, and to evolve histories of its changing usage.

The current state of the discipline of literary studies is one where there is considerable debate concerning basic questions of terminology. This involves, among other things, the boundaries which distinguish the literary from the non-literary; the position of literature within the larger sphere of culture; the relationship between literatures of different cultures; and questions concerning the relation of literary to other cultural forms within the context of interdisciplinary studies.

It is clear that the field of literary criticism and theory is a dynamic and heterogeneous one. The present need is for individual volumes on terms which combine clarity of exposition with an adventurousness of perspective and a breadth of application. Each volume will contain as part of its apparatus some indication of the direction in which the definition of particular terms is likely to move, as well as expanding the disciplinary boundaries within which some of these terms have been traditionally contained. This will involve some re-situation of terms within the larger field of cultural representation, and will introduce examples from the area of film and the modern media in addition to examples from a variety of literary texts.

ACKNOWLEDGEMENTS

Many friends and colleagues have helped, inspired and supported me during the writing of this book. In particular I would like to thank Desmond Graham, Michael Rossington, and Anne Whitehead. Ruth Helyer gave me invaluable help in compiling the glossary. The conversations that I have had with Trev Broughton over many years go on influencing my thinking about autobiography. Ann Spencer has cheered me up and cheered me on during the writing of this book and I am grateful to her for all her support. John Drakakis has been an assiduous and wise editor. I am also grateful to my editor at Routledge, Liz Thompson, for her patience and encouragement.

INTRODUCTION

All biographies like all autobiographies like all narratives tell one
story in place of another.

(Helene Cixous, *rootprints*, p.177)

It is my **political** right to be a subject which I must protect.

(Roland Barthes, *Camera Lucida*, p.15)

AUTHORS AND SUBJECTS

'Autobiography is indeed everywhere one cares to find it', Candace
Lang wrote in 1982, thus acknowledging a major problem for
anyone who studies this topic: if the writer is always, in the broadest
sense, implicated in the work, any writing may be judged to
be autobiographical, depending on how one reads it (Lang 1982: 6).
However, autobiography has also been recognized since the late
eighteenth century as a distinct literary genre and, as such, an
important testing ground for critical controversies about a range of

ideas including authorship, selfhood, representation and the division between fact and fiction. The very pervasiveness and slipperiness of autobiography has made the need to contain and control it within disciplinary boundaries all the more urgent, and many literary critics have turned to definitions as a way of stamping their academic authority on an unruly and even slightly disreputable field. Philippe Lejeune considered the problems, and in 1982 produced the following judicious and widely quoted definition:

> A retrospective prose narrative produced by a real person concerning his own existence, focusing on his individual life, in particular on the development of his personality.
>
> (Lejeune 1982: 193)

However, Lejeune himself remained dissatisfied with this since it did not seem to provide a sufficient boundary between autobiography and the adjacent genres of biography and fiction. A certain 'latitude' in classifying particular cases might be admitted but one condition for autobiography was absolute: there must be 'identity between the *author*, the *narrator*, and the *protagonist*' (Lejeune 1982: 193). However, the difficulty is how to apply this condition since the 'identity' Lejeune speaks of can never really be established except as a matter of *intention* on the part of the author.

As a recent critic of autobiography, Laura Marcus, has noted, the concept of 'intention' has persistently threaded its way through discussions of autobiography (Marcus 1994: 3). Attacked by the New Critics of the 1930s and 1940s as a fallacy, 'intentionality' signals the belief that the author is behind the text, controlling its meaning; the author becomes the guarantor of the 'intentional' meaning or truth of the text, and reading a text therefore leads back to the author as origin. Within critical discussions of autobiography, 'intention' has had a necessary and often unquestioned role in providing the crucial link between author, narrator and protagonist. Intention, however, is further defined as a particular kind of 'honest'

intention which then guarantees the 'truth' of the writing. Trust
the author, this rather circular argument goes, if s/he seems to be
trustworthy. Hence for Roy Pascal, an early critic of the genre, autobiography depends on 'the seriousness of the author, the seriousness
of his personality and his intention in writing' (Pascal 1960: 60).
For Karl Weintraub, an autobiography can only be understood if
the 'place' the authors themselves occupy in relation to their lives
can be reconstructed by the reader. Reading an autobiography
'properly' means reading with an already existing knowledge of
the text's meaning: 'This moment, this point of view, needs to be
recaptured for a proper understanding of the autobiographic
effort; so must the motivation and intention of the author for
writing autobiography at all' (Weintraub 1978: xviii). For these
critics, autobiographies are seen as providing proof of the validity
and importance of a certain conception of authorship: authors who
have authority over their own texts and whose writings can be read
as forms of direct access to themselves (Olney 1972: 332). Even
Philippe Lejeune, with whom we started, and for whom the concept
of the author is more difficult to define, requiring him to resort
to 'authoritative' legal terminology, proposes an 'autobiographical
pact' or 'contract' based on 'an intention to honour the signature'.
According to Lejeune, the author of an autobiography implicitly
declares that he is the person he says he is and that the author
and the protagonist are the same (Lejeune 1982: 202); but have
we necessarily believed all subjects in the same way? Have all sig-
natures had the same legal status? Does not sincerity itself, as Nancy
Miller suggests, already imply a masculine subject, since women
are less likely to be believed simply on account of who they are
(Miller 1988: 51)?

   Miller's argument demonstrates the extent to which the genre of
autobiography has been implicitly bound up with gender. Insofar
as autobiography has been seen as promoting a view of the subject
as universal, it has also underpinned the centrality of masculine –
and, we may add, Western and middle-class – modes of subjectivity.

As we shall see, by focusing on a particular historical canon of texts which celebrated the extraordinary lives of 'great men', an important group of modern critics writing in the 1960s and 1970s deduced abstract critical principles for autobiography based on the ideals of autonomy, self-realization, authenticity and transcendence which reflected their own cultural values. For James Olney, for instance, autobiography engages with a profound human impulse to become both separate and complete:

> What is . . . of particular interest to us in a consideration of the creative achievements of individual men and the relationship of those achievements to a life lived, on the one hand, and an autobiography of that life on the other is . . . the isolate uniqueness that nearly everyone agrees to be the primary quality and condition of the individual and his experience.
>
> (Olney 1972: 20–1)

By gesturing towards a shared truth which 'everyone' can endorse, Olney establishes a particular view of the individual as transcending both social and historical difference. An appeal to the mysteries of the self can also function in much the same way as a mystificatory rhetoric obscuring the ideological underpinnings of its particular version of 'selfhood'. According to Karl Weintraub, man's task is, like autobiography's, to arrive at some form of self-realization: 'We are captivated by an uncanny sense that each one of us constitutes one irreplaceable human form, and we perceive a noble life task in the cultivation of our individuality, our ineffable self' (Weintraub 1978: xiii). As individuals, 'we', as Weintraub says, assuming that 'we' represents everyone, are above society and beyond understanding; by implication, therefore, 'we' are also beyond the reach of any theoretical critique.

It seems that there is little apparent difference for these critics between realizing the self and representing the self, and autobiography gets drawn seamlessly into supporting the beliefs and values of an essentialist or Romantic notion of selfhood. According to this view, generated at the end of the eighteenth century but still powerfully present in the middle of the twentieth, each individual possesses a unified, unique selfhood which is also the expression of a universal human nature. For Olney, for instance: 'the explanation for the special appeal of autobiography . . . is a fascination with the self and its profound, its endless mysteries' (Olney 1980: 23). At the same time, however, autobiography, understood in terms of a similarly transcendent or Romantic view of art, is turned to in the first place because it offers an unmediated and yet stabilizing wholeness for the self. Autobiography exemplifies 'the vital impulse to order' which has always underlain creativity (Olney 1972: 3). Or it offers the possibility of alleviating the dangers and anxieties of fragmentation: 'Autobiography . . . requires a man to take a distance with regard to himself in order to constitute himself in the focus of his special unity and identity across time' (Gusdorf, in Olney 1980: 35). Autobiography, as we shall see, has sometimes been viewed as aiding the diversification of culture and subjects through its appeal to different communities, its formal multiplicity and its excessive productivity. In the 1960s and 1970s, however, it was reinscribed by literary critics as itself offering a solution to the same threat it had posed by being restricted to the literary values of the 'few' and made to take on a unifying and conservative function.

Returning for a moment to definitions, we can see a revealing paradox at work in this formative criticism of the 1960s and 1970s. On the one hand, autobiography is perceived to be as ineffable and irreducible as the self it figures: 'Definition of autobiography as a literary genre seems to me virtually impossible', writes James Olney (1972: 38). On the other hand, critics like Lejeune and Gusdorf believed that the form must provide both 'conditions and limits' if it is to be containable and identifiable as an authoritative form of 'truth-telling' which is clearly distinguishable from fiction (Gusdorf, in Olney 1980). On the one hand, autobiography, through its relation to individualism and humanistic values, is seen to be available to non-technical, common-sense readings: according to Barett Mandel, 'Every reader knows that autobiographies and novels are finally totally distinct' (Mandel 1980: 54). On the other hand, autobiography produces an unease that it could spread endlessly and get everywhere, undermining even the objective stance of the critic if it is not held at bay or constrained by classification.

Candace Lang has argued that criticism and autobiography are difficult to separate, since they are both self-conscious discourses '"about" language' and thus engaged in the same task (Lang 1982: 11). Robert Smith makes a similar point when he sees autobiography as 'a good way of taking the theoretical temperature . . . of academics in the field' (Smith 1995: 59). For the group of critics we are dis-cussing here, the apparent neutrality or 'liberalism' of their approach to the subject both disguised and supported their critical authority. Autobiography was important to them because it helped to shore up an approach to the meaning of literary works through the author. The critic could have 'objective' knowledge of the work, thus ratifying their own place and authority, precisely because auto-biography could be seen to supply a subjecthood which was both ineffable and discrete. The author stood behind the work guaran-teeing its unity, while the critic interpreted what the author really meant to say, reducing the different elements of a work to a central message. What happens to autobiography afterwards, after the theoretical temperature hots up, forms the main substance of this book. Autobiography has been at the centre of the debates, which, drawing on mainly French theories of psychoanalysis, post-structuralism and feminism, have interrogated the self-evident nature of the subject and knowledge. Poststructuralism, in particular, by positing language or discourse as both preceding and exceeding the subject, deposed the author from his or her central place as the source of meaning and undermined the unified subject of autobiography. For the moment, however, before engaging more fully with these ideas and their relation to autobiography, I want to pose the problem of genre in more historical terms.

THE LAW OF GENRE

The term 'autobiography' is commonly thought to have been coined by the nineteenth-century poet Robert Southey in 1809 when he was describing the work of a Portuguese poet, Francisco Vieura; however, there is evidence of slightly earlier usage, at the end of the eighteenth century, in a review attributed to William Taylor of Isaac D'Israeli's *Miscellanies*, where he ponders whether 'autobiography', though 'pedantic', might not have been a better term than the 'hybrid' word 'self-biography' employed by D'Israeli (Nussbaum 1989: 1; Marcus 1994: 12). Felicity Nussbaum argues that by the 1830s the word had become a matter of established usage, though definitions of what it might mean were by no means stable. From her perspective, focusing on a range of eighteenth-century autobiographical writing, the pressure to read these texts in conformity with 'dominant notions of a unified self' comes later, indeed can be dated to the more prescriptive approach to autobiography adopted by those modern critics we have aready discussed and who derived their models from a few 'classic' texts (Nussbaum 1989: 4–5). According to Laura Marcus, the nineteenth century saw a gradual alignment of autobiography with the value accorded to authorship. If one of the anxieties around early discussions was the public exposure of the private self, it is also the case that autobiography gradually comes to be the site where genius, and in particular literary genius, could be established as 'internally' valuable, without reference to other 'outside' judgements. The writer had a vocation which was not to be determined or valued in terms of the market-place, but only with reference to the self. Taking Wordsworth and Carlyle as her two exemplars of nineteenth-century autobiography, Mary Jean Corbett sees how for them, 'writing autobiography becomes a way of attaining both literary legitimacy and a desired subjectivity' (Corbett 1992: 11). Autobiography resituates the writer *in* his work, thus mitigating the dangers of the anonymity and the alienation of modern authorship: 'The presence of his signature, the narrative unfolding of his history, inscribes the text as belonging to Wordsworth, who becomes "knowable" to his readers and inseparable from this text as a function of that self-representation' (p.40).

Vocation would seem to be the key to authorship and it is also the way in which 'serious' autobiography, that written by the few who are capable of sustained self-reflection, is to be distinguished from its popular counterpart. It is still the case today that popular, 'commerical' autobiographies by, for instance, pop stars are often seen as lacking 'integrity', as debasing the self by commodifying it. For nineteenth-century critics, such populism could be seen to threaten the respectability of the form. For one reviewer, writing in 1829 in *Blackwoods Magazine*, there was, quite explicitly, 'a legitimate autobiographical class' which excluded the 'vulgar' who try to 'excite prurient curiosity that may command a sale'. Autobiography should rather belong to people of 'lofty reputation' or people who have something of 'historical importance' to say (Marcus 1994: 31–2). Social distinctions were thus carried across into literary distinctions, and autobiography was legitimized as a form by attempting to restrict its use. By the nineteenth century there was a definite hierarchy of values in relation to self-representation with memoirs occupying a lower order since they involved a lesser degree of 'seriousness' than autobiography. As Laura Marcus puts it: 'The autobiography / memoirs distinction – ostensibly formal and generic – is bound up with a typological distinction between those human beings who are capable of self-reflection and those who are not' (p.21). Similarly, autobiography came to be equated with a developmental narrative which orders both time and the personality according to a purpose or goal; thus the looser, more chronological structure of the journal or diary could no longer fulfil this 'higher' function of autobiography. According to Clifford Siskin, 'development' in the nineteenth century becomes 'an all-encompassing formal strategy underpinning middle-class culture: its characteristic way of representing and evaluating the individual as something that grows' (Siskin 1988: 12). However, to return to Felicity Nussbaum's point, such a view comes later, and it would be wrong to see earlier eighteenth-century writers of journals and diaries as 'failing' to write developmental narratives. Instead, what they found 'most "natural" was . . . something that recounted public and private events in their incoherence, lack of integrity, scantiness and inconclusiveness' (Nussbaum 1989: 16). The writing and rewriting of the self over a period of time, through constant revisions or serial modes, which was common across a range of autobiographical forms and writers before the nineteenth century, confounds the notion that there is one definitive or fixed version. What we must take account of, there-fore, is the way a developmental version of the self, which is also socially and historically specific, has come to provide a way of interpreting the history of the genre: all autobiography, according to this universalizing and prescriptive view, is tending towards a goal, the fulfilment of this one achieved version of itself.

The question that is posed by the above discussion is not simply what kind of genre is autobiography; it is rather how does the 'law of genre', to take the title of Jacques Derrida's famous essay, work to legitimize certain autobiographical writings and not others? According to Derrida, it is in the very notion of a genre to consitute itself in terms of 'norms and interdictions': 'Thus, as soon as genre announces itself, one must respect a norm, one must not cross a line of demarcation, one must not risk impurity, anomaly or monstrosity' (Derrida 1980: 203–4). However, it is also part of Derrida's argu-ment that every time a text designates itself as belonging to a genre – calls itself an autobiography, for instance – it does so through a statement which is not itself autobiographical. Hence a title which refers to a text as an 'autobiography' does not itself belong to the genre of autobiography. This may seem like a rather pedantic point, but it leads Derrida to conclude that there is always 'an inclusion and exclusion with regard to genre in general' (p.212) and that no text can actually fulfil its own generic designation. What is at stake here for Derrida is not the power of individual texts to transgress the law of genre but rather the way the law of genre can only operate by opening itself to transgression. As we shall see, Derrida's point is also part of his larger questioning of the borders of the text, of what belongs to the 'inside' and the 'outside'. His writing engages again and again with the impossibility of stabilizing texts from the outside, since all markers of the 'outside', such as the title and signature, will get drawn into the process of the text's engendering. In attempting to posit a higher level of generality, genre is necessarily too general, but it is also never general enough.

Fredric Jameson has also questioned the ability of a genre to operate as a 'law'; instead he sees genre as unable to detach itself from what it is meant to define: 'Genres are so clearly implicated in the literary history and formal production they were traditionally supposed to classify and neutrally to describe' (Jameson 1981: 107). For Celeste Schenk, Jameson's argument has suggested the way genres are always 'cultural constructions themselves' and operate not as 'ideal types' but as 'overdetermined loci of contention and conflict' (Schenk, in Brodski and Schenk 1988: 282). However, it is also the case that for Jameson genre has a more pragmatic function in that it will be one of the ways writers will use to try to ensure that their text is received and read appropriately: 'No small part of the art of writing, indeed, is absorbed by this (impossible) attempt to devise a foolproof mechanism for the automatic exclusion of undesirable responses to a given literary utterance' (Jameson 1981: 106–7). The markers of genre can thus be used to insist on a resemblance to what is already known, and to organize and regulate the meanings of a text for the reader.

Genre could thus be seen as a way of creating a dynastic relation between texts, encoding tradition in formal features which operate like 'family characteristics'. According to Alastair Fowler's more positive view of genre, genre works beneficially by building a tradition of similar texts through a kind of genealogical imperative. Each work, according to Fowler, 'is the child . . . of an earlier representative of the genre and may yet be the mother of a subsequent representative' (Fowler 1982: 32). If we go back to Derrida's essay, we can see that Derrida had also perceived how genre has a 'controlling influence' on 'that which draws the genre into engendering, generations, genealogy, and degenerescence'. However, according to Derrida, this also reveals how the question of genre can never be posed simply as a formal one:

> It covers the motif of the law in general, of generation in the natural and symbolic senses . . . of the generation difference, sexual difference between the feminine and masculine genre/ gender . . . of a relationless relation between the two, of an identity and difference between the feminine and the masculine.
> (Derrida 1980: 221)

He also points out that in French there is a different range of meaning for the term, that 'the semantic scale of genre is much larger' and 'always includes within its reach the gender' (ibid.). In other words, genre cannot avoid calling up gender through semantic proximity; indeed as Alastair Fowler unwittingly demonstrates, in the lexical and metaphorical passage of genre through generations, sexual difference is inevitably installed at its heart: families descend through mothers as well as fathers, though it may be only the father's line that can claim to be legitimate. Mary Jacobus argues, with reference to Alastair Fowler's notion of a generic 'family', that 'genre is always impure, always "mothered" as well as fathered' (Jacobus 1989: 204). Citing Derrida, she invokes his paradoxical idea of the law of genre as 'a principle of contamination, a law of impurity' (Derrida 1980: 206). As we shall see, feminist critics have perceived the politics of genre at work in its turn towards a patriarchal law which delegitimizes women's writing. However, the writing of women, or perhaps of any subject who is deemed to be different, allows us to read back into genre the heterogeneity or transgressive-ness it tries to exclude. Genre, according to Derrida, assigns us 'places and limits': 'I have let myself be commanded by . . . the law of genre', he writes (p.227). Autobiography, we could say, turns itself into a genre in order to 'place' the subject, the 'I', only to be undone by the instability and difference already instated within the law.

POSTSTRUCTURALIST INTERVENTIONS

In 1979, Paul de Man published a radical essay on autobiography entitled 'Autobiography as De-Facement', in which he signalled the end of autobiography. Autobiography, de Man argued, was 'plagued' by a series of unanswerable questions, which arose from the fundamental attempt to conceive of autobiography as a separate genre at all. According to de Man, autobiography 'always looks slightly disreputable and self-indulgent' in the company of the major genres – the novel, poetry and drama – never quite attaining aesthetic dignity nor even providing an empirically useful way of understanding texts since 'each specific instance seems to be an exception to the norm' (de Man 1979b: 919).

Most important of all for de Man, however, is the problem that is encountered as soon as one attempts to make a distinction between fiction and autobiography, and finds oneself taken up in the whirligig of 'undecidability', inhabiting a threshold between contradictory ideas. This experience, in de Man's words, is like being 'caught in a revolving door': you never get out of the dilemma but merely suffer from the increasing effects of vertigo (de Man 1979b: 921). As his own alternative point of departure, de Man proposes that autobiography is not a genre at all but 'a figure of reading or understanding' that is in operation not only within autobiography but also across a range of texts. He identifies autobiography with a linguistic dilemma which is liable to be repeated every time an author makes himself the subject of his own understanding. The author reads himself in the text, but what he is seeing in this self-reflexive or specular moment is a figure or a face called into being by the substitutive trope of prosopopoeia, literally, the giving of a face, or personification. The interest of autobiography, according to de Man, is that it reveals something which is in fact much more generally the case: that all knowledge, including self-knowledge, depends on figurative language or tropes. Autobiographies thus produce fictions or figures in place of the self-knowledge they seek. What the author of an autobiography does is to try to endow his inscription within the text with all the attributes of a face in order to mask or conceal his own fictionalization or displacement by writing. Paradoxically, therefore, the giving of a face, prosopopoeia, also names the disfigurement or defacement of the autobiographical subject through tropes. In the end there is only writing.

De Man illustrates his thesis with reference to Wordsworth's *Essays Upon Epitaphs* (1810); not surprisingly, since it is part of his point that autobiography always contains the epitaphic, that it posits a face and a voice that speaks to us, as it were, beyond the grave. For de Man, the 'trope' that allows autobiography to speak also carries contradictory signs of death:

> 'Doth make us marble,' in the *Essays upon Epitaphs*, cannot fail to evoke the latent threat that inhabits prosopopoeia, namely that by making the death speak, the symmetrical structure of the trope implies, by the same token, that the living are struck dumb, frozen in their own death.
>
> (De Man 1979b: 928)

Language both gives a voice and takes it away. In an earlier, companion essay to this one, 'Time and History in Wordsworth', de Man had commented that *The Prelude* was an 'epitaph written by the poet for himself', even if it was difficult 'to imagine a tombstone large enough to hold the entire *Prelude*' (de Man, in Chase 1993: 63). In this long autobiographical poem, who speaks to us is a dead man, addressing us, as it were, from his own tombstone. In *Essays Upon Epitaphs*, the deaf Dalesman is seen by de Man as Wordsworth's evocative figure for the plight of language: 'Language, as trope, is always privative. . . . To the extent that, in writing, we are dependent on this language we all are, like the Dalesman in the *Excursion*, deaf and mute' (de Man 1979b: 930). The Dalesman, called up by language to conceal its own silence – the silence ultimately of the grave – also carries the repressed sign of that silence. The human figure is after all also figured by the silent text. This is the dilemma of autobiography for de Man: to call up a figure for the self which is by the same token a 'disfiguring', to depend for its 'life' on the same textual figure that contains the sign of its death: 'Autobiography veils a defacement of the mind of which it is itself the cause' (ibid.).

De Man's essay constitutes a supremely deconstructive moment for Romantic selfhood, quite literally turning its assumptions on their head: instead of a subject who is unique, unified and transcendent, the Romantic self – post-de Man – is fatally divided, threatened by representation, forced to summon up rhetorically the ghosts of a self they can never hope to be. As Robert Smith writes, remarking on this significant turning point in autobiographical theory: 'As soon as language becomes an issue . . . any last footing "the autobiographical subject" may have had gives way' (Smith 1995: 58). The subject is undermined by metaphor, dissolved into words. The 'I', on which both the subject's and autobiography's identity had depended, is now seen as referring not to a subject but to its own placing as a signifier within language or in a chain of signifiers. 'The death of the author' which Roland Barthes had announced in 1968, and which signalled his attack on the concept of the author as origin or source of meaning, also had implications for autobiography. Just as Barthes saw the author as 'linguistically . . . never more than the instance writing', so he sees the 'I' as 'nothing more than the instance saying I' (Barthes, in Rice and Waugh 1989: 116). The pre-existing subject of autobiographical theory and its stabilization within a genre that could, like the self, be identified and recognized, was presented as an illusion, unmasked. Were we also then witnessing the death of autobiography?

The problem with death when it is invoked rhetorically, as it frequently is within poststructuralist theory, is that it is never quite the end, and leaves space for all kinds of ghostly returns. To go back to de Man for a moment, the notorious discovery in 1987, after his death, of his wartime journalism in a Belgian collaborationist newspaper, including an anti-Semitic article entitled 'The Jews in Contemporary Literature', dramatically changed how de Man was read. As Geoffrey Galt Harpham writes: 'De Man's work suddenly switched genres, being read now not as literary criticism but as a coded testimony' (Harpham 1995: 390). Some critics tried to interpret de Man's work as a complicated, lingering act of expiation through which he was producing the analytic tools that would have enabled him to cut through the subjective mystification he had succumbed to in his youth. Others saw de Man's undermining of authorial responsibility and voiding of autobiographical self-hood as driven by personal necessity: his own need to repress his past. Paradoxically, his very departure from autobiography in his writing is what causes it also to return. In retrospect, too, the obsessive figures of falling, mutilation and drowning, which pervade his criticism, and which he offers as figures for the defacement of writing by tropes, could also be read as more darkly personal images of anxiety and guilt, concealing another reference point in his own life.

The violent irruption of autobiography into theory which this disclosure of de Man's past has seemed to represent to many critics may cause us to question a purely textual model of reading such as de Man proposed. However, as Shoshana Felman warns us, there is no easy way to locate the historical referentiality of writing. Whereas de Man thought that, at the time, his wartime journalism was simply 'factual', a form of historical witnessing, it is later shown, through historical hindsight, to have been involved with the 'ideological fiction' of fascism. However, fiction can also have 'real consequences': 'That history subverts its witnessing and turns out to be linguistically involved with fiction does not prevent the fiction, however, from functioning historically and from having deadly factual and material consequences' (Felman 1993: 147). In other words, history is never safely 'out there', to be defined in opposition to fiction, but instead can, at any time in the future, disrupt our understanding; nor is fiction free as Felman says 'from real effects' which can work independently of their intent (p.148). Ultimately, for Felman, de Man's silence about his past tells us about the impossibilty of simply remembering or representing trauma: his silence is also a testimony; it *addresses* us by reminding us of our own collusion in this silence, the repression of the past (p.164).

So far as autobiography is concerned, the usefulness of post-structuralist theory for our understanding of it continues to be debated. The argument that texts can have political or historical effect revives the question of referentiality or truth, without neces-sarily returning us to the same place. Indeed the notion of multiple locations, both as contexts of reading and positionings for the subject, becomes one of the ways autobiography has offered itself as a site for new theoretical and critical insights. Robert Smith suggests that 'as a field of interpretation, autobiographical criticism and theory is . . . conflictual and miscellaneous' (Smith 1995: 58). One could also say that it is both productive and diverse.

This book looks at some of the debates surrounding autobiography as well as taking acccount of the complex relationship between the theory and practice of autobiography. In Chapter 1, I write about some of the texts which have made up the 'great tradition' of auto-biographical writing: Saint Augustine's *Confessions*, Bunyan's *Grace Abounding*, Rousseau's *Confessions* and Wordsworth's *Prelude*. What is at issue is both the development of a narrative for the self which has been constructed partly by later readings and which stresses the similarities between texts, and the more discontinuous history which emerges when autobiography is seen as a site for negotiating and challenging the different ways meaning is given to the self. This chapter already introduces poststructuralist theory as it is; arguably, only when this lens becomes available can we denaturalize the unitary or Romantic subject and see it as a historical instance, involved in its own ideological strategies. In Chapter 2, I focus on poststructuralist theory and in particular the work of Sigmund

Freud, Jacques Lacan, Roland Barthes and Jacques Derrida, all of whom in different ways undermined the assumptions of humanism and posited instead a divided subject, debarred from self-knowledge by the unconscious or by language. All four also move between theoretical writing and autobiography as if what causes knowledge of the subject to disperse also brings about the dispersal of the subject into knowledge. The subject and object of knowledge are no longer divisible, able to be thought of separately. In Chapter 3, I look at autobiographical writing, in particular by female and postcolonial subjects, which has interrogated the ideological underpinning of autobiographical tradition and explored the possibility of difference as excessive and uncontainable, not able to be recuperated to any notion of a 'norm'. This chapter also asks how autobiography can be used or read as a mode of political questioning at the very juncture of contradictory and dissonant discourses. Finally, in Chapter 4, I return to some of the issues raised by this Introduction; in particular, the relationship between autobiography and criticism and the ethical value of autobiography as a form of witnessing or testimony, which, however, can never overcome the problem of where to locate the past.

1

HISTORIANS OF THE SELF

SAINT AUGUSTINE'S *CONFESSIONS*

In this chapter I want to look at some of the texts which have helped to form the dominant tradition of autobiographical writing and the way they have both drawn on and helped to construct a history of selfhood, a paradigmatic narrative through which the subject has learned to know who s/he is.

The best place to begin is with Saint Augustine's *Confessions* (*c.* AD 398–400) which is often thought of as the origin of modern Western autobiography, both in the sense of marking a historical beginning and of setting up a model for other, later texts. Georg Gusdorf, one of the important modern critics of autobiography whom we discussed in the Introduction, sees the *Confessions* as 'a brilliantly successful landmark' within a historical landscape he has already limited to 'our cultural area', and defined as both Western and Christian. According to Gusdorf, autobiography requires a kind of consciousness of self which is 'peculiar to Western man'. Augustine's *Confessions* express 'in full rhetorical splendour'

the Christian imperative to the confession of sins and thus promote
that inward-turning gaze which is the origin and basis of autobiography (Gusdorf 1956: 29, 31). Roy Pascal's interest in the
Confessions is even more generically focused and generalizing than
Gusdorf's. This 'first great' autobiography has a 'decisive significance', he argues, in that it establishes a crucial narrative design
where incidents, trivial in themselves, become representative
moments in the growth of a personality. The author does not so much
remember the past as recast it, grasping and reshaping himself
in the process, and it is, according to Pascal, through creating
this 'integrated succession of experiences' that the *Confessions* lift
autobiography into art (Pascal 1960: 22–3). For another early critic
of autobiography, Karl Weintraub, who announces at the beginning
of his book that he is searching for 'that proper form of autobiography' in which 'a self-reflective person asks "who am I?" and
"how did I become what I am?"', the *Confessions* also hold a special
position. None of the 'ancient' writers before him, Weintraub argues,
though they might have written autobiographically, had 'opened up
their souls in the inwardness of genuine autobiography'; moreover,
Augustine creates a model, partly through his own understanding
of the typicality of his experience, which will be influential for
centuries to come (Weintraub 1978: 1, 45).

What seems to be at stake in all these early critical approaches
to Augustine's *Confessions* is the definition of autobiography as a
genre. By isolating Augustine's text from his classical predecessors,
the criteria which define autobiography can themselves begin to
be isolated (Misch 1907, Vol. 1: 17). The historical moment of
the *Confessions* is both refigured and repeated as the inaugurating
moment of autobiography. As Jonathan Dollimore says, it is difficult
to see Augustine as occupying any single point in history since
the characteristics of his narrative have completely infused the
way we structure our understanding of him; he is continually
'scripted' in terms of the same narrative he himself 'powerfully influenced' (Dollimore 1991: 131). The *Confessions* discredit the past and

re-form it in terms of a meaning which transcends history, and therefore help to establish a critical narrative of autobiography as a genre which is also 'beyond' history. In approaches to the *Confessions*, critical and autobiographical subjects crucially reflect and reinforce each other. What we see is the unified subject of modern liberal ideology successfully allegorizing their own history.

At a simple level, the *Confessions* tell the story of Saint Augustine's conversion to Christianity. This involves a process of spiritual and physical wandering, as Augustine charts his development from babyhood to manhood and a journey which takes him from his birthplace in Thagaste, in North Africa, to Carthage where he taught rhetoric, to Rome and then Milan where his conversion finally happens. The notion that his wanderings should also be read as the tribulations of error is introduced early on:

> I was still my own unhappy prisoner, unable to live in such a state yet powerless to escape from it. Where could my heart find refuge from itself? Where could I go, yet leave myself behind? Was there any place where I should not be a prey to myself? None. But I left my native town. For my eyes were less tempted to look for my friend in a place where they had not grown used to seeing him. So from Thagaste I went to Carthage.
>
> (Augustine 1961: 78)

As his biographer Peter Brown has suggested, the *Confessions* are a 'strictly intellectual autobiography' and 'a manifesto of the inner world' (Brown 1967: 167–8). By turning towards the outside world Augustine believed he was also losing himself, and as a result losing sight of God. 'You were there before my own eyes, but I had deserted even my own self. I could not find myself, much less find you' (Augustine 1961: 92). The outward journey is a false journey, becoming meaningful only in retrospect by being realized as a return: it is a tortuous journey back to God. The narrative thus merely defers a resolution which, from another perspective, is already known. This other perspective, of course, could be God's. Towards the end of the *Confessions* Augustine meditates on the 'vast cloisters' of memory where he 'meets himself' (p.215); memory is the container of his experiences, necessarily lived in time, but memory also exists beyond time and comprehension: it is greater than what it contains. 'This means, then, that the mind is too narrow to contain itself entirely. . . . Is it somewhere outside itself and not within it? How, then, can it be part of it, if it is not contained in it?' (p.216). Augustine's 'transcendent' relation to his own memory is analogous to God's relation to his Creation: Augustine searches for God within his memory but God is also 'above' him, the timeless container of all human destinies. 'In the same way you are not the mind itself, for you are the Lord God of the mind. All these things are subject to change, but you remain supreme over all things, immutable' (p.231). The *Confessions* conflate Christian and narrative imperatives: Augustine's conversion also has to be read as a conversion, in narrative terms, to a point of view from which the future, now become past, can be seen as part of the overall design. Augustine becomes god-like in his ability to read the formless or inconsequential events of his life in terms of their eventual meaning (Sturrock 1993: 20–48).

Two incidents from the *Confessions*, one about sin or a fall from truth, the other about redemption, will allow us to elaborate the argument further. In the first episode Augustine famously recounts his boyhood theft of some pears. What seems particularly shameful in retrospect about this apparently minor episode is its sheer wilfulness. He steals the pears neither from need nor greed: the fruit is in itself not particularly 'enticing' and few of the pears actually get eaten. Rather, Augustine describes himself as delighting in transgression for its own sake. 'Let my heart now tell you what prompted me to do wrong for no purpose, and why it was only my own love of mischief that made me do it' (Augustine 1961: 47). Two aspects of this incident seem significant: first, Augustine does not act alone but as a member of 'a band of ruffians' (ibid.). The gregarious energy of youth seems tantamount to sinfulness in itself: the laughter and 'fun and games' generated by the group induce a reckless disregard for the law which would never have been tolerated by Augustine alone. This helps to highlight the contrary movement of the *Confessions* towards singleness and individuality: sin can be committed in company, but salvation requires a private and increasingly inward kind of soul-searching. The second feature of this incident emphasized by Augustine is its contingency and pointlessness. Sin is thought about in terms of wasteful energy – it is a waste of time – diverting him from the path of Truth. It is also a detour, a digression, in terms of the direction his story is taking. 'Can anyone unravel this twisted tangle of knots?' Augustine asks at the end of this section (p.52), deep in the entanglements of his story, and his sins, yet anticipating the clarity of their resolution (absolution).

The second episode, the moment of Augustine's conversion, seems significantly to repeat the first, for the final conversion also happens in a garden and uses as its context a children's game. Augustine, at the climax of a long period of indecision, first removes himself physically from company, and then even from his faithful friend Alypius who has followed him into the garden. It is at this point that he hears a child chanting 'tolle lege' or 'take it and read' and chooses to interpret the dislocated words not as part of a forgotten child's game but as a divine command (Augustine 1961: 177). He picks up the Bible and selects at random a verse from Paul's Epistle to the Romans: 'Not in revelling and drunkenness, not in lust and wantonness, not in quarrels and rivalries. Rather, arm yourselves with the Lord Jesus Christ; spend no more thought on nature and nature's appetites' (p.178). This speaks so directly to his own weaknesses that it confirms for him an act of heavenly intervention and dispels his final doubts.

It is easy to see the ways in which this episode both echoes and redeems the earlier one. The child's voice, which *could* have been taken as an accidental coincidence, hearkening back to a world of frivolity and play, is now transferred or converted into a higher realm of meaning; the passsage extracted from the Bible, which Augustine, in effect, appropriates for himself, is likewise read as a form of direct address, yielding an instantaneous meaning. The divine imposes its order on the secular as the word, removed from the fallibility of human interpretation, becomes the Word, the divine Logos. This garden marks both a return and a new beginning.

Just before this turning point, however, Augustine has had a vision of Continence, in all her 'chaste beauty', but 'not barren', 'a fruitful mother of children, of joys born of you, O Lord, her spouse' (Augustine 1961: 176). Continence is precisely what he has found so difficult to espouse himself and with it the renunciation of marital and sexual fulfilment. Her apparition is a supreme moment of conflict for Augustine – 'I wrangled with myself, in my own heart' (p.177) – and turns him decisively in on himself: 'I probed the hidden depths of my soul and wrung its pitiful secrets from it' (ibid.). According to John Sturrock, this moment of inner turmoil is what the *Confessions* realize at length: 'This highly emotional moment of the story ranks as a *mise en abyme* of the work as a whole. Augustine is launched on the path of confession' (Sturrock 1993: 44). Augustine therefore records here, in a condensed or metaphorical way, what will be repeated in a kind of hall-of-mirrors effect throughout the *Confessions*.

Yet it might also be possible to argue at this point that Augustine is encountering some of the most intractable issues arising from autobiography as a genre. As we have seen, Paul de Man has argued that it is precisely the 'specular moments' when an author becomes the subject of his own understanding that he must also depend on the trope or rhetorical figure of prosopopoeia or personification. He gives language a face at this moment of self-recognition as a way of avoiding his own implication in language, only to be confronted once again by the inevitably rhetorical nature of language (de Man 1979a: see pp. 13–15 of this volume). Continence's attempt to shield Augustine from fleshly temptation by interposing her own body into the text is not dissimilar, in its paradoxical force, to her figurative character being used to mask the duplicitous nature of language.

Augustine's dilemma as an autobiographer is how to get through language to a state of transcendent unity with himself while writing in a language which works through material signs and thus introduces the inevitable effects of duration, the time required by the *process* of reading, and uncertainty. This is true even of his conversion in the garden: while he attempts to transfigure both spoken and written texts, the child's words and Paul's Epistle into a divine message, the very form of his conversion tells of their more mundane origin as texts. Avrom Fleishman has pointed out that there are various literary motifs at play in the conversion scene, including the vision, the children's game, and the *sortes*, or opening of a privileged text at random, which derive from Jewish, pagan and Christian traditions, all of which would have been well known to Augustine as a teacher of rhetoric. This for Fleishman suggests that 'his experience at the turning point of his life was *from the moment itself* an act of literary interpretation' (Fleishman 1983: 54). For T.R.Wright, as well, the conversion is an extremely 'intertextual conversion' which involves 'a complex chain of conversion narratives'. The story of Ponticianus' conversion which precedes Augustine's own has itself been effected by reading the life of St Anthony who was himself influenced by a passage from the Bible (Wright 1988: 95–6). If conversion follows conversion, we could equally say that story succeeds story in an endless act of reading and reinterpretation.

Augustine's struggle with language is also enacted in the dual address of the *Confessions*. Written in the vocative – using 'you' – they have as their direct addressee God. But as Augustine himself asks, what is the point of telling God what He, in his omniscience, already knows? 'O Lord, since you are outside time in eternity, are you unaware of the things that I tell you? Or do you see in time the things that occur in it? If you see them, why do I lay this lengthy record before you?' (Augustine 1961: 253). For Augustine, the answer is that he is also writing his *Confessions* for men, who in the position of overhearers or witnesses will be able to learn from his life and to share his vision of God. Augustine is aware that there are two problems about his *Confessions*: first, how will people know that he is telling the truth, and second, how can he 'confess' without also offering up his life for judgement by others? By making God his addressee, Augustine also claims Him as the arbiter of his truthfulness (it is impossible to lie to God) and as his supreme reader: 'It is you, O Lord, who judge me' (p.210). By being face to face with God, Augustine creates a saving space or division between human and divine responses; he can be humble in his attitude to God while taking on god-like power to prescribe how his life should be interpreted. 'I shall therefore confess both what I know of myself and what I do not know. For even what I know about myself I only know because your light shines upon me' (p.211). However, it is his human reader who in the end justifies his *Confessions* since it is for his sake that Augustine must set out his life in time as a history or as a narrative, in the form of words. As Jean Starobinski has argued: 'The double address of the discourse – to God and to the human auditor – makes the truth discursive and the discourse true' (Starobinski 1971a: 78). The story in all its literality can ultimately offer the only approach to its own desired dissolution into a higher and wordless form of truth.

It is to the question of God's position as transcendent interlocutor, a God who knows everything in advance, that Jacques Derrida returns, from a poststructuralist perspective, in his commentary on the *Confessions* in his own autobiographical text 'Circumfession'. Derrida reads Augustine contrary to or against what Augustine says as wanting something more than truth, and it is this desire for *more*, some chance, some unpredictable event 'as though Augustine still wanted, by force of love' that 'something should happen to God' (Derrida 1993: 18) that the *Confessions* enact for Derrida. At the same time Derrida draws attention to the fact that Augustine writes his confessions after the death of his mother, and like Derrida himself, could be said to be writing *for* his mother. But that *for* has its own twists: it could mean both towards and in her place. The *Confessions* do indeed move relentlessly towards Augustine's mother Monica.

It is Monica who urges him on to conversion and it is with Monica, after his conversion, that he shares a sublime and wordless vision of the eternal life:

> And while we spoke of the eternal Wisdom, longing for it and straining for it with all the strength of our hearts, for one fleeting instant we reached out and touched it. Then with a sigh, leaving our *spiritual harvest* bound to it, we returned to the sound of our own speech, in which each word has a beginning and an ending – far, far different from your Word, our Lord, who abides in himself for ever, yet never grows old and gives new life to all things.
>
> (Augustine 1961: 198)

Augustine and his mother must return to the transitory world, but for Monica this moment of fusion (with God and each other) marks the end of her life and for Augustine the beginning of his own spiritual, and autobiographical, authority. After her death there is nowhere else to go; no further progess to be made. Augustine, having transcended bodily desires and attachments, addresses himself not to his mother but to God.

However, if Augustine's text moves towards the death or elimination of the other person, in this context the mother, our own reading perhaps does not need to, but can recognize instead the importance of the mother within the structure of the autobiography. This is the point which Nancy Miller makes. For her the representative masculine subject of autobiography, for which the *Confessions* have seemed to offer such an important paradigm, is built upon readers simply following Augustine's lead and taking Augustine's final position as the text's summation; they have re-suppressed the mother's role which Augustine nevertheless draws attention to until almost the end of his text. For Miller this is part of a larger argument about the gendering of autobiography. What has been widely assumed, since feminist criticism of the 1970s, to be a female model of the self as defining itself through relations with others, may also, she argues, apply to male texts, forcing us 'to revise the canonical views of male autobiographical identity altogether' (Miller 1994: 5). I will return to feminist criticism of autobiography more fully in the next two chapters. For the moment, however, we can begin to see Augustine's writing as never attaining the final mastery of truth he desires but as haunted by its own otherness, by figures of its own uncertainty or dissolution. For Derrida confession necessarily broaches something unclosable, something which can never be laid to rest, something that exceeds rationality. From this point of view we should not be surprised if behind the rhetorical figure of Continence that we looked at earlier we can glimpse the more immediate, emotive and mortal figure of the imploring mother. Nor that the tears that Augustine failed to shed at his mother's death – 'when the body was carried out for burial, I went and returned without a tear' (Augustine 1961: 201) – should well out of the text at every turn. Indeed tears carry the body back into the text in a melancholy, abject streaming. The paradox of Augustine's text, for all its centrality in establishing the unified, transcendent 'I' of autobiographical tradition, may be that for the 'I' to see and to turn its gaze self-consciously both inwards and upwards, it must first be blinded by tears, it must reveal its dependence on the very body it abjures. As Derrida has provocatively noted: 'A work is at once order and its ruin. And these weep for one another' (Derrida 1990: 122).

NON-CONFORMING SELVES: JOHN BUNYAN'S *GRACE ABOUNDING*

Seventeenth-century England, particularly the period after 1640, witnessed an extraordinary outpouring of spiritual memoirs and autobiographies. One important reason for this was the breakdown of state censorship during the civil war and a newly democratized access to print culture (Delany 1969: 81). For members of the dissenting sects which proliferated during this period, and who produced by far the largest number of such autobiographies, personal testimony was an important form of religious propaganda. 'Mechanick preachers' like John Bunyan who lacked institutional sanction or formal education for their ministry, instead founded their authority on a personal account of their special calling and journey towards grace (Bunyan 1962: xxix). Indeed after 1660, when dissenting preachers began to be subjected to periodic but intense persecution, this positioning of the dissenting subject beyond the state became a more openly defiant and individualized gesture (Nussbaum 1989: 70). Bunyan wrote his autobiography, *Grace Abounding to the Chief of Sinners* (1666) after he had been imprisoned in 1660, for being, as he states there, 'an Upholder and Maintainer of unlawful Assemblies and Conventicles, and for not conforming to the National Worship of the Church of England' (Bunyan 1962: 95). This period of imprisonment was to last twelve years, though with occasional and tantalizing reprieves.

Like Augustine's, Bunyan's narrative takes its form from the experience of spiritual conversion, though there is nothing to suggest that Bunyan was directly influenced by, or indeed had even read, the *Confessions*. However, what Puritan selfhood shared with the Augustinian model of the *Confessions* was an emphasis on a search for unity with God which could redeem the self's sinfulness and hence its incoherence. According to the historian Christopher Hill, the profound effect of the Reformation had been 'to leave the believer and his conscience alone in the world with no help except from divine grace' (Hill 1986: 23). The Puritan subject must turn inwards, reliant solely on his own conscience, a divine injunction addressed to him alone. The most important relation for a Puritan, subsuming all others in their 'infinite variety' was, according to Perry Miller, 'the relation of the individual to the One'. 'If man once achieved knowledge of God and of his soul, the answer to all other questions would soon follow' (Miller 1939: 8). Moreover, since evil was also the self's responsibility, the Puritan must both strive to separate himself from his own fallen state and punitively keep watch over his own erring soul. The meaning of life depended on a rigorous separation of the soul from the contamination of sin, good from evil. This profound dualism can be seen as fuelling both confession and conversion.

For Bunyan, like Augustine, therefore, it is the spiritual implications of the events of his life that are significant. Retrospectively he picks out those which reveal a providential design – how, for instance, he was spared from various accidents and survived the war – or illustrate his extreme sinfulness, later to be redeemed by 'the merciful working of God upon my Soul' (Bunyan 1962: 5). One of these early stories, his playing of a game of Cat (bat and ball but played with pieces of wood) is not unlike Augustine's stealing of pears, in that the spiritual significance that he reads into it seems to far exceed the seriousness of the exploit itself. Here, in the middle of his game, Bunyan hears a divine voice telling him to choose between Heaven and Hell. Looking up, he sees as if 'with the eyes of my understanding . . . the Lord Jesus looking down upon me, as being very hotly displeased with me, and as if he did severely threaten me with some grievous punishment for these, and my other ungodly practices' (p.10). It is a profoundly individualizing moment, since Bunyan alone of the group of playmates is picked out for this dire warning. It is also a moment when the spiritual impinges on the empirical world, transforming a game into a lesson, and making guilt the necessary consequence of play.

Yet, however much he is forced to confront a Divine meaning, Bunyan's conversion never quite takes the authoritative and conclusive form of Augustine's. For one critic, Robert Bell, Bunyan is simply 'never as sure as Augustine'. This he attributes to the 'Puritan view of things, forever poised between hope and despair' (Bell 1977: 118). The very need constantly to separate oneself from sin suggests both the fluidity of the boundary, and an anxiety that such a division may leave one finally and irreparably on the wrong side. Again and again in *Grace Abounding* we see Bunyan return to a state of searching and uncertainty, in a struggle for salvation which is both arduous and ongoing. 'O the combats and the conflicts that I did then meet with!' (Bunyan 1962: 60), Bunyan laments at one point, as he sees his certainty dissolve 'sometimes twenty times a day' (p.64). As he himself writes in the Preface, his story develops repetitively, oscillating between his 'castings down, and raisings up' (p.2). Bunyan's progress depends upon repeated backsliding, and the hope, rather than the certainty, that conversion has already taken place. In the words of John Calvin, the elect must 'employ their whole life in the exercise of repentance, and know that this warfare will be terminated only by death' (Hawkins 1980: 272). Bunyan's spirituality is both effortful and unconsummated. While Augustine raises his eyes to Heaven and is released into tears, Bunyan's internal 'warfare' involves a corresponding strain upon his body. 'By the very force of my mind in labouring to gainsay and resist this wickedness my very Body also would be put into action or motion, by way of pushing or thrusting with my hands or elbows' (Bunyan 1962: 42). The body, though intrusive, is here labouring with the mind rather than against it; later, however, Bunyan's spiritual progress and the parting from his wife and children is imagined in terms of the most painful of physical rendings, 'pulling the flesh from my bones' (p.98). Bunyan was reluctant to give up, if not sensuality, then the immediacy of his physical life (p.116). This accounts for the often noted concreteness of his vision, the detail in the foreground which pulls our attention away from his spiritual quest towards his more homely dwelling. Bunyan often provides a literal or metaphorical 'house' for his vision, noting, for example, in one important providential meeting that the poor women of Bedford were sitting 'at a door in the sun' (p.14) or imagining Jesus looking 'down from Heaven through the Tiles upon me' (p.65). If, for Augustine, the body makes a return, leaking its pain and passion into his text, for Bunyan it is never relinquished, but jostles for attention alongside the ordeals of his soul.

    Grace Abounding is both didactic and exemplary. As with Augustine's *Confessions*, readers have frequently taken Bunyan's text, even though there are important differences between the two, as an enduring model of spiritual struggle and conversion. Its popularity, both in Bunyan's lifetime and the century after, is attested to by the huge number of later editions and translations. However, its transcendence as a text of its historical moment has been partly enabled by Bunyan's own detaching of his spiritual life from history. He makes only a passing reference to the Civil War and says little about the specific reasons for his imprisonment. It is also supported by Bunyan's realism which convinces the reader how personal and yet how *ordinary* the experience is. Bunyan himself, in the Preface, points to the unmediated nature of his writing which he compares with the unadorned and authoritative nature of divine intervention. 'God did not play in convincing of me; the Devil did not play in tempting of me . . . wherefore I may not play in my relating of them, but be plain and simple, and lay down the thing as it was' (Bunyan 1962: 3–4). More ingenuously, he later remarks how 'I never endeavoured to, nor durst make use of other men's lines . . . for I verily thought, and found by experience, that what was taught me by the Word and Spirit of Christ, could be spoken, maintained, and stood to' (pp.87–8). The extent to which Bunyan's text is conventional, drawing both on patterns and formulations of experience which he shared with other writers of the period, as well as echoing, in particular, Martin Luther's writing, has been widely commented on (Haskin 1981: 302–3; Tindall 1934: 30). The paradox of Bunyan's autobiography is that he can assert its originality in the face of an apparent conventionality, even, indeed, because of it.

Luther is comfortably accommodated within *Grace Abounding* as confirming the importance of Bunyan's own experience rather than influencing it. Delighting in his fortuitous discovery of an old book, *Luther's Commentarie on the Galatians*, he comments:

> I found my condition in his experience, so largely and profoundly handled, as if his Book had been written out of my heart; this made me marvel: for thus thought I, this man could

not know anything of the state of Christians now, but must
needs write and speak of the Experience of former days.

(Bunyan 1962: 41)

Any anxiety about Luther as a historical precursor is held in check
by Bunyan making his own experience pre-date his discovery of
Luther. Indeed even the Bible, Bunyan's weightiest pre-text, exists
in *Grace Abounding*, less as a source for his writing than as something
which happens to him experientially; bits of text 'dart', 'rowl in',
'boult' or 'fall' upon his soul, beyond, as it were, his own volition,
and his turning to the Bible is most often a later need to verify the
Word which he has already received directly and internally. The
Puritans, having substituted individual experience for the institutional and legal authority of the Established Church, were left
with the problem of how to prove that their own subjective experience was indeed what they said it was, direct communication with
God. As we have seen, the burden of doubt is felt by Bunyan as
he struggles to attain an impossible certainty and create a unified
subject position for himself. The only available 'proof' or verification
was the degree to which individual experience conformed to an
already established pattern. Bunyan anxiously surveyed his own soul
but he already knew what he was looking for. As Peter Carlton has
noted in general of Puritan 'lives': 'The pattern they were taught,
they sought for; the pattern they sought, they experienced' (Carlton
1984: 29). This circularity meant that the uniqueness and directness
of Bunyan's experience served to mask its conventionality; but
equally it was only by its coincidence with other such spiritual
journeys that he could maintain its authenticity.

Despite its contradictions, *Grace Abounding* seemed to offer its
readers, then and later, the model of a unified private selfhood
which had divine authority. Arguably, it is this private self, now secu-
larized, which will serve the needs of a newly emergent middle
class in the period to come, producing a coherent claim to identity
in the place of ideological conflict (Nussbaum 1989: 37–8). What

has been established at the same time, however, is the elision of conformity with nonconformity; this model binds a belief in the individual as a free agent with unique access to his own inner self to the practice, which has more to do with the establishment of an ideological and social cohesiveness, of scrutinizing and regulating the self.

SERIAL SELVES: JAMES BOSWELL AND HESTER THRALE

Bunyan attributed an important role to his wives in *Grace Abounding*: it is his first wife who begins to awaken his 'desire to religion', and passes on to him important religious texts which had been left her by her father (Bunyan 1962: 8). He makes the parting from (presumably his second) wife and children when he is imprisoned one of the supreme tests of his religious faith. However, this does little more than confirm women in a subsidiary position, by making them aids, hindrances or witnesses to Bunyan's own progress towards salvation. It would be wrong to assume, however, on the basis of *Grace Abounding*, that this was necessarily women's role in the period. Seventeenth-century women also wrote conversion narratives, having been given access to equal subjecthood by the belief within certain radical sects that the distinction between good and evil superseded all others, including, even, the differences between men and women (Graham *et al.* 1989: 3). These narratives, just as those written by men, were thought of either as private exercises, an attempt to assess the subject's progress towards salvation, or as public models, published, often posthumously, and offered by the male clergy to other sectaries as example or treatise. As we have seen with *Grace Abounding*, therefore, the writer could find validity and importance for herself, but only within a framework of already prescribed experiences and emotions. Yet women's negotiations with these narratives were not always completely smooth, and tensions can be perceived as they move between the expectations of the genre and of their own feminine role. Sara Davy, for instance, in her posthumously published *Heaven Realized* (1670), may seem to reveal to a modern reader not just the conventional story of her sinfulness and salvation, but the more intimate complications of guilt at her brother's death, suppressed anger with her mother and intense love for another woman (Graham *et al*. 1989: 165–79), while Anne Wentworth, in her *Vindication* (1677), defends her right to leave her husband, her 'hardhearted yoke-fellow', even to publish things to his 'prejudice and scandal' because of the higher claims of her 'heavenly bridegroom' (Graham *et al*. 1989: 180–96). While these autobiographical writings constructed the subject through strict narrative and linguistic conventions in order to create a conforming, if transcendent, version of selfhood, for women they could also offer an alternative space, a place from which to contest their socially sanctioned position of silence and submission.

The argument that some autobiographical genres, such as the conversion narrative, privilege the masculine subject must always be held in check, therefore, by a recognition of the different and historically variable uses that can be made of such narratives. This argument also applies, though now in reverse, to the presumed compatibility between women's experience and the informal and repetitive narratives of diaries and journals. Some recent critics believe that diaries have had a particular importance for women, allowing them to become authors in private, and thus circumvent a historical prohibition. For others the 'female form' of the diary created a space where the traditional ordering of narrative and meaning could begin to be undone. According to Annette Kolodny, 'the fine distinctions between public and private, or trivial and unimportant, which served as guides for the male autobiographer have never really been available to women' (Kolodny, in Jelinek 1980: 240–1). The unchronological and unprogressive form of the diary could be viewed, therefore, as a reflection of women's different experience, or as a deliberate strategy, an escape into a potential or protean form of subjectivity. What then of diaries written by men?

In the seventeenth and eighteenth centuries, the diary had become a popular form as literacy expanded and as the authority of both Church and State receded. Journals were private and increasingly secular documents where the individual could broach the question of their everyday life instead of being urged, in emulation of the Divine example, to transcend it. For James Boswell, who wrote and rewrote his life in notes and journals, and who eventually, with his 'peculiar talent for abridging' (Boswell 1950: 332), assembled them in his monumental biography, *The Life of Johnson* (1791), attention to detail was seen not only as a way of preserving experience against the effects of time and forgetfulness, but of keeping the mind constantly under review. The diary was an *aide-mémoire*, to be turned to retrospectively when 'remembrance' had faded (Boswell 1970: 307), but it was also justified artistically as registering a freshness and authenticity of impression which might be lost in subsequent retelling. Boswell's account of Johnson, for which he copiously reproduced his notes of conversations between them, was, he considered, unique for this reason: mankind was enabled 'to see him live, and to "live o'er each scene" with him'. According to Boswell, 'had his other friends been as diligent and ardent as I was, he might have been almost entirely preserved' (Boswell 1970: 22).

However, the diary was also a 'register of one's life', by which Boswell meant it was a place to return to in order to contemplate one's self, or one's 'character', otherwise unregarded in the disturbance and confusion of living: 'It is very necessary to have our thoughts and actions preserved in a mode not subject to change, if we would have a *fair* and distinct view of our character' (Boswell 1951: 330). Boswell considered that there was perhaps 'more pleasure in reflecting' than living (Boswell 1950: 40) and that life which had not been recorded would inevitably become dispersed and lost: 'Sometimes it has occurred to me that a man should not live more than he can record, as a farmer should not have a larger crop than he can gather in' (Boswell 1951: 332). It was this serious dimension to the journal, as an access to the moral knowledge of 'character', that protected

Boswell's journal writing from the charge of triviality and allowed it to be a 'manly' pursuit. According to the contemporary view, it was women who, immersed in the domestic and the private, attended to 'minute particulars' while men took charge of the public narratives of history and philosophy (Nussbaum 1989: 202). Boswell, guarding against the feminization of his writing, caustically drew a distinction between the self-regarding gaze of the woman and the intense self-scrutiny of the male: 'And as a lady adjusts her dress in the mirror, a man adjusts his character by looking at his journal' (Boswell 1970: 898). Boswell here claims the journal as a serious, and (consequently) masculine, form of self-reflection.

Yet by summoning up the mirror analogously, he also introduces a gap or division into his idea of the self between the surveying consciousness and the self surveyed. The subject, according to Boswell, looks to the journal in order to see a self which is not always the same: the private reflection may not fit the public gaze. The diary becomes the place where he can examine and discard aberrant identities:

> When my father forced me down to Scotland, I was at first very low-spirited, although to appearance very high. I afterwards from my natural vivacity endeavoured to make myself easy; and like a man who takes to drinking to banish care, I threw myself loose as a heedless, dissipated, rattling fellow who might say or do every ridiculous thing. This made me sought after by everybody for the present hour, but I found myself a very inferior being.
>
> (Boswell 1950: 62)

This 'looseness' of character, unacceptable as much for its unpredict-ability as for any particular weaknesses, is very different from the character Boswell 'chooses' to adopt. 'I was now upon a plan of study-ing polite reserved behaviour' (Boswell 1950: 61); later, almost as if he were picking a character off the peg, he asserts, 'I felt a strong disposition to be a Mr Addison' (p.62). In the privacy of his journal

Boswell can admit not only to faults of character, but to an instability which turns his choice of a 'proper' character into the adoption of another, possible dramatis personae. Publically, however, Boswell argued for a necessary stability: 'Nothing is more disagreeable than for a man to find himself unstable and changeful . . . In proportion therefore as the intellectual faculties are exalted, will the character be fixed' (Boswell 1951: 325). The journal was the private repository for those errant selves which proved inconsistent with the public character, and which must be labelled 'out of character' in order to maintain the 'truth' of the public self. Public character could be 'fixed' because the journal could contain and restrain any problematic 'looseness'.

In writing his *Life of Johnson* (1791), Boswell could be seen to be resolving many of his problems with 'character', achieving a tentative reconciliation, within the character of Johnson himself, of that uneasy division between the public and private self (Nussbaum 1989: 117). Formally, the *Life* is woven out of many different kinds of discourse: Johnson's diaries, letters and conversations as well as Boswell's own notes, journals and intermittent commentary. As we have seen, Boswell justified the inclusiveness of the *Life* on the grounds of realism. However, Boswell also argued that all the details ultimately cohere because all serve to illuminate further his 'illustrious subject': 'they are all in some degree connected with him' (Boswell 1970: 7). By writing the life of another, Boswell can unify and make meaningful that which is episodic and incidental; he can convey the 'real' meaning of the details from a position of knowledge. Throughout the *Life*, Johnson's 'character', while it is allowed to have 'imperfections' and contradictions, nevertheless emerges as a superior being who rises to eminence through his innate qualities of mind and spirit, rather than rank or wealth. He is 'manly' (Boswell 1970: 69), endowed with 'transcendent powers' (p.86), and an 'inflexible dignity of character' (p.94), whose reason always masters both melancholy and imagination (p.49); in other words, he is made to exemplify a human or humanistic ideal of character where constancy and self-mastery are 'natural' features. Boswell has constructed the model of character that he needs, and to which he can claim proximity through both friendship and writing.

Significantly, though Boswell presents Johnson as a universal subject whose humanity transcends both class and history, he also clearly characterizes him as masculine. His precocious 'manliness' is evident, according to Boswell, when, as an infant, he feels 'insulted' by his schoolmistress' protectiveness and beats her 'as well as his strength would permit' (Boswell 1970: 30). Later mysogynistic comments are also eagerly recorded, as in the famous comparison of a woman's preaching to 'a dog's walking on his hinder legs' (p.327). That masculinity required this aggressive beating off of the feminine is evident in Boswell's policing of his own version of Johnson against other memoirists. In particular it is Mrs Thrale (later Piozzi) who figures in the *Life*, sometimes anonymously as 'a lady', who threatens the 'reasonableness' of Boswell's account, and whose accuracy Boswell calls into question. Represented as fanciful and therefore undisciplined, she is reprimanded by Johnson himself, in Boswell's account, for 'little variations in narrative' which 'deviate' from the notion of 'truth' conceived of, by Johnson, as an absolute. 'It is more from carelessness about truth than from intentional lying, that there is so much falsehood in the world' (p.899). Boswell will solicit the 'impartial reader' to discount her 'small volume' of Johnson's sayings as unrepresentative: here it is less the accuracy of her recall that is under attack than her judgement. Truth requires fairness and moderation, an assimilation of all the detail into a unified view. The 'harshness of demeanour' which Mrs Thrale's book seems to demonstrate comprises instances, according to Boswell, which were spread over years; years 'in which his time was chiefly spent in instructing and delighting mankind by his writings and conversation, in acts of piety to God, and good-will to men' (pp.290–1). Truth, it appears, is an elastic and largely ideological construct which excludes both feminine 'fancy' and contradictory facts. Boswell carefully positions the reader as sharing the general and universal 'truth' about Johnson while Mrs Thrale's account, in drawing attention to Johnson's peculiarities, is itself made to take on the qualities of singularity and deviancy.

Ironically, it was Johnson himself who first encouraged Mrs Thrale to keep a journal, bestowing the same encouragement on her that he had on Boswell. That Hester Thrale owed the beginnings of her private and prolific journal writing not only to Johnson, but also to her husband's gift of blank notebooks, is testimony to the ambiguity of her diary, even when kept secretly, as an alternative and yet compliant feminine discourse, produced with, and perhaps for, the approval of men. Her writings were also 'dignified' by being, in part, a repository for the sayings of Johnson, and it is these, rather than her more domestic writing, that were published in her lifetime: her *Anecdotes of the Late Samuel Johnson* (1786) were followed by the publication of *Letters to and from the Late Samuel Johnson* in 1788. Her public literary identity was therefore as the confidante of a great literary man.

Yet Thrale was also alert to her own 'difference' as a writing woman, who, however much she might admire and try to emulate literary men, was also situated as female in a domestic sphere which made heavy demands upon her. She could never be quite the assiduous recorder of Johnson that Boswell was because her time and attention were otherwise taken up:

> All my friends reproach me with neglecting to write down such Things as drop from him [Johnson] almost perpetually, and often say how much I shall some Time regret that I have not done't with diligence ever since the commencement of our Acquaintance: They say well, but ever since that Time I have been the Mother of Children, and little do these wise Men know or feel, that the Crying of a young Child, or the Perverseness of an elder, or the Danger however trifling of any one – will soon drive out of a female Parent's head a Conversation concerning Wit, Science or Sentiment, however She may appear to be impressed by it at the

> moment: besides that to a *Mere de famille* doing something is more necessary & suitable than even hearing something; and if one is to listen all Even and write all Morning what one has heard, where will be the Time for tutoring, caressing, or what is still more useful, for having one's Children about one.
>
> (Thrale 1942: 158)

This reads both as a justification for her own shortcomings as memoirist and a spirited defence of her different priorities: 'the Mother of Children' both knows and feels things which 'wise Men' do not.

Yet for all her motherly attentiveness, Thrale was an inveterate note keeper. From 1776 to 1809 she kept what she called her *Thraliana*; never intended as a consistent diary, it contains anecdotes, quotations, literary opinions and pieces of personal history in imitation of the French tradition of 'ana', as the collecting together of fragments of these kinds was known (Thrale 1942: xi). These writings allowed her to position herself in terms of diverse discourses without having to strive for consistency, to partake of literary models in an oblique and intermittent way while 'modestly' discounting her own literary ambitions. She saw it as composed of 'scraps', 'madly selected' and 'awkwardly put together' (p.840). 'For Nonsense and Whim – long live the *Thraliana*', she wrote in 1777, just a year after its inception (p.134). Unedited and unrevised, it was 'a sort of literary Curiosity', as was the draft of Pope's Homer:

> We have got a sort of literary Curiosity amongst us; the foul Copy of Pope's Homer, with all his old Intended Verses, Sketches, emendations &c. strange that Man shd keep such Things! – stranger still that a Woman should write such a Book as this; put down every Occurrence of her Life, every Emotion of her Heart, & call it a *Thraliana* forsooth – but then I mean to destroy it.
>
> (Thrale 1942: 464)

Significantly she goes on to disagree with Dr Johnson's estimate of the interest of reading Pope's rough drafts by comparing it to an act of male voyeurism: 'a malicious Pleasure Such as Men feel when they watch a Woman at her Toilet' (ibid.). Clearly, her writing, if it were ever made public in its naked state, would be even more at risk from the salacious interest of men. However, she did not, as she asserts, destroy it and even on occasion allowed herself to toy with the idea of future readers, helpfully offering them an explanation on one occasion 'lest it should be wholly unintelligible' (p.229). Serving as a kind of written accompaniment of her life – 'my Confident, my solitary Comfort, and Depositary of every thought as it arose' – the *Thraliana* is also bound up with her fears of mortality and hopes of survival: 'What will be done with my poor *Thraliana* when I am dead' (p.799). The writing seems to occupy a space so close to the physical body that it is doubtful whether it can have an autonomous existence. If the notion of other readers raised the spectre of a violating masculine gaze, Thrale's secret relationship with her writing can suggest an almost maternal protectiveness to its textual body.

All-inclusive as the *Thraliana* may seem in its range of interests, it is not, however, the only journal writing that Thrale undertook. She also kept a 'Family Book' which she began in 1766 initially as a 'memorandum' of the growing abilities of her first daughter 'Queenie', but which gradually expanded to become a domestic history of all her children's births, progress, ailments and deaths – Hester Thrale bore twelve children, only four of whom survived into adulthood. Her views on her role as wife and mother were on the whole conservative: she accepted her 'duty' in a loveless marriage as bearer of children and particularly of male heirs. Yet the 'Family Book' is in many ways a radical document, in its discourse around motherhood and its revealing of Thrale's powerful role as educator as well as nurturer of her children; she continually records all her children's attainments and failures, both mentally and physically, with an astuteness and care for their individuality. In 1777 she wrote the following assessment of the differences between her four daughters:

> Susan is really surprising when one recollects her beginning; & She is exceedingly clever . . . but is special ill Tempered to be sure, tho' I think her Health can hardly be mended
>
> Sophy is a fine Countenanced well proportioned Girl, of a good disposition and as *the old Phrase* was of a towardly Wit: Cecilia is lively & forward of her Months, and bids fair to be a bit of a Beauty like her eldest Sister. Hetty was always inclinable to be sandy and so is She, but Hetty has been always exceedingly admired – I wish poor Cicely may have half her Share.
>
> (Hyde 1977: 179)

In the domestic sphere, Thrale was allotted care of the body, and this extended beyond her children to the men of the household as well. Dr Johnson came to her to be nursed through his illnesses and while her husband only visited her two or three times a week after the birth of their first child 'in a sort of formal way' (Thrale 1942: 308), she prepared and applied poultices to his infected testicle after he contracted venereal disease. The irony of the situation was not lost on her: 'I now began . . . to perceive that my poor Father's Prophecy was verified who said If you marry that Scoundrel he will catch the Pox, & for your Amusement set you to make his Pultices' (Hyde 1977: 166). Yet it would be wrong to see her role as nurse as simply demeaning. She continually asserts her expertise against male physicians, disputing both their diagnosis and treatment, and positions herself powerfully in terms of the discourses of the body and illness. It was Thrale's role not only to give birth to the children but to preside over their education, their well-being, their health and, most poignantly, their deaths. Traditionally, women have been given the function of 'being' the body within masculine discourse, of being both the silent ground or material base of thinking and disruptive other which must be expelled in order to preserve the integrity of reason. Thrale's 'Family Book' offers an alternative discourse of maternal watchfulness, where the body also signifies – it is a system of signs to be read – and is interwoven with, rather than opposed to, rational identity. Boswell's battle with Thrale over how Dr Johnson should be written about is also a battle over what constitutes the human subject. For Boswell, reason alone ensured the subject's wholeness. Thrale's 'Family Book' however, instead reveals, with remarkable clarity and control, the discontinuity and complexity of lives necessarily lived in and through the physical body.

SUBLIME EGOS: ROUSSEAU AND WORDSWORTH

Jean Jacques Rousseau's *Confessions*, which he completed in 1770 and which were published posthumously between 1781 and 1789, seem to hark back, through the title at least, to Saint Augustine. Yet, according to many commentators, Rousseau, instead of following previous spiritual models, was ushering in, through this prodigiously sustained, even obsessional self-writing, a new model of secular autobiography for the Romantic era. According to Huntington Williams, Rousseau both exemplifies 'modern Romantic autobiography' and occupies a 'pivotal' position in its historical development. Rousseau's refusal of other sources for himself and 'radical internalization' of personal identity makes him, for Williams, both 'novel' and 'influential' (Williams 1983: 3). W.J.T. Mitchell sees Rousseau as 'the great originator' and 'the first modern man', a writer whose reputation and thinking permeated the nineteenth century to such an extent that one did not necessarily have to have read him to be influenced by him: 'simple literacy', according to Mitchell, 'was enough' (Mitchell 1990: 648).

The attribution of originality to Rousseau by these critics echoes, of course, the view promulgated by Rousseau himself; he famously heralds the *Confessions* with the confident assertion of his own singularity:

> I have resolved on an enterprise which has no precedent, and which, once complete, will have no imitator. My purpose is to display to my kind a portrait in every way true to nature, and the man I shall portray will be myself.
>
> Simply myself. I know my own heart and understand my fellow man. But I am made unlike any one I have ever met; I will even venture to say that I am like no one in the whole world. I may be no better, but at least I am different. Whether Nature did well or ill in breaking the mould in which she formed me, is a question which can only be resolved after the reading of my book.
>
> (Rousseau 1953: 17)

Though in the very next paragraph Rousseau goes on to invoke a 'Sovereign Judge' and an 'Eternal Being', God is being given only a peripheral role to play: Rousseau addresses God as a source of emphasis at the beginning of his autobiography rather than turning to him, either here or elsewhere, as a pre-eminent and sufficient arbiter of a truth. Truth for Rousseau becomes conflated with truthfulness, the non-verifiable *intention* of honesty on the part of the author. Truth, therefore, can never be established once and for all, but can only be presented in terms of the constant reiteration of avowals and disclaimers by Rousseau himself. Rousseau transposes to 'man', and, in particular, 'natural man' or Nature, the power to know or see inside the self that once resided with God. There is, for Rousseau, no higher form of knowledge than feeling; self-knowledge, it soon becomes evident, is inseparable from conviction or intuitive self-understanding, from 'a knowledge of his heart' that belongs to him alone. 'I have only one faithful guide on which I can count; the succession of feelings which have marked the development of my being' (Rousseau 1953: 262). Without recourse to Divine help, or intervention, situated within secular time, Rousseau's 'feelings' stretch out into a succession of endlessly renewable inner revelations about himself. His 'self' is plotless and, because it is without climax or denouement, seemingly interminable. Rousseau,

having completed the *Confessions*, will embark on other autobiographical projects, the *Dialogues* (1776) and the *Reveries* (1778).
The 'truth of feelings', forever renewing and repeating itself in the
present, is also never complete.

Rousseau believed his task as autobiographer was to tell or
'confess' all and make himself as transparent to his readers as he was
to himself. 'I must leave nothing unsaid' he reminds himself in
Book Twelve (Rousseau 1953: 548). His autobiography was less an
attempt to remember the past, to memorialize the life he led, than
to make others recognize the inner truths about himself that he
already knows through the unique access he has to his own feelings:
'Throughout the course of my life, as has been seen, my heart
has been as transparent as crystal, and incapable of concealing for so
much as a moment the least lively feeling which has taken refuge
in it' (p.415). As Jean Starobinski says, Rousseau would have liked
to offer himself as 'an open book' to the reader, to reveal his feelings
without shadow or obliquity. It was only the reader's unwillingness
or obtuseness which made this impossible (p.181). Transparency
for Rousseau pre-existed writing; it was what the writing aspired
to return to, but it was also created by the writing through the
unstinting attempt to offer proof to the reader and make himself
clear:

> I should like in some way to make my soul transparent to the
> reader's eye, and for that purpose I am trying to present it from
> all points of view, to show it in all lights, and to contrive that
> none of its movements shall escape his notice, so that he may
> judge for himself of the principle which has produced them.
>
> (Rousseau 1953: 169)

Ultimately, Rousseau believed that if the reader came to the wrong
conclusion it would be his own fault. His responsibility as autobiographer was to give the reader all the evidence that was available;
all, therefore, that the reader should need in order to arrive at the

correct judgement. Though the truth may be immediate and spontaneous, its communication to the reader, on the other hand, must be prolonged and insistent. 'It is not enough for my story to be truthful', Rousseau writes; 'it must be detailed as well' (ibid.).

From the start, therefore, Rousseau is caught up in a series of paradoxes or contradictions in relation to his autobiographical project, and it is perhaps not surprising that his 'history' or story tells of repeated incidents where he finds himself powerless to act, the victim of a plot that repeatedly turns against him. Rousseau cannot simply 'dwell in the grace of transparency', to use Jean Starobinski's phrase (Starobinski 1971a: 182); he must articulate and prove himself through 'confession'. Despite himself, he therefore becomes trapped in the mediating power of story and language, and the 'plot' of his autobiography could well be seen as displacing on to the outside world the connivances and designs which belong, at least in part, to autobiographical writing itself. Rousseau, according to John Sturrock, is the 'arch catastrophist' among autobiographers, punctuating his narrative with 'doleful markers' of the fateful turn that events are about to take (Sturrock 1993: 141). One such moment comes when, as a boy of 15, he fails to get back to Geneva before the drawbridge is raised. 'When I was twenty paces away I saw them raise the first bridge. I trembled as I watched its dreadful horns rising in the air, a sinister and fatal augury of the inevitable fate which from that moment awaited me' (Rousseau 1953: 49). Instead of extolling his ensuing bold choice of freedom, Rousseau dwells on the obstruction placed in his way: he sees himself, both here and elsewhere in his text, as the victim of external events. Fate, it seems, imposes a life on him through such arbitrary yet crucial and often malign turns; Rousseau, on the other hand, is passive, since whatever he does has already been determined by a previous event over which he had no control. Alone and without power to act except as fate determines, Rousseau cannot be blamed. While the external world and other people are untrustworthy and have proved to be duplicitous, if not downright vindictive, he is, above all, innocent, and his autobiography is as much his 'alibi' as it is his confession (Starobinski 1971a: 194).

Given that his problems all stem, according to Rousseau at least, from his relation with the external world, with other people, the oppposite also turns out to be the case: Rousseau is at his happiest when he can escape into an unbounded state of reverie, when he can wander and think without encountering limit or obstruction. Early on, he embraces a life of vagabondage, a picaresque existence, and it often seems that his mind can range freely when his body is also free to roam: 'There is something about walking which stimulates and enlivens my thoughts. When I stay in one place I can hardly think at all, my body has to be on the move to set my mind going' (Rousseau 1953: 158). At these moments, 'thrown into the vastness of things', as he says, he can think 'without fear or restraint'. He can 'dispose of all Nature as its master' (ibid.). These are also times when Rousseau is free to absorb the outer into the inner world, when the subject is 'master', and when the 'plot', which is necessarily an ongoing story of encounters and frustrations, is temporarily suspended.

Yet if Rousseau derives most happiness from his own company, when he places himself at a distance or excludes himself from society, it is also, in part, because he already feels himself to be excluded. Socially he is a poor man, without status or family to protect him. He has no special significance or importance in terms of his rank or wealth. Part of the point of his autobiography is to claim his right to be heard despite his social inferiority, to assert another 'natural' order which gives priority to inner qualities of mind and feeling and according to which his own distinction will be recognized. Far from being indifferent to other people, Rousseau is using his auto-biography as a form of coercion, as an attempt to put right both social and personal sleights and misrepresentations and to prove his own specialness, his apartness. Under threat of misapprehension, Rousseau must speak out, he must, in John Sturrock's words, 'spread the truth about himself so as to bely the slanders of others' (Sturrock

1993: 153). As Rousseau embarks on the second part of the *Confessions* he feels increasingly beset by derision; the truth which should be sufficient is, Rousseau fears, never enough. In a sense he is progressively invaded by his own fictionalized construction of the Other, the projection of all that threatens him, which his truth fails to keep at bay. 'Being forced to speak in spite of myself, I am also obliged to conceal myself . . . The ceiling under which I live has eyes, the walls that enclose me have ears' (Rousseau 1953: 263). Wanting to tell the truth in all its immediacy, Rousseau is forced into concealment; separating himself from others, he installs them again in his text through the very act of writing. Rousseau's delusion is to believe he could either totally absorb others into his own self-image or reject them. As his fictional self-image expands to fill the world, he retreats inside it; others, now re-created in the form of phantasmal presences, become, paradoxically, even more threatening, since they can easily pass through the flimsy walls of his self, monitoring and judging him from the inside.

The question of why Rousseau arrived at such a distorted sense of human relations begs a further question: What purpose did it serve for him? Rousseau himself relates his loss of trust in others to an incident in his childhood. Wrongly accused of breaking a comb when he is boarding with Pastor Lambercier and his sister, he refuses to confess and is repeatedly beaten: 'They were unable to force from me the confession they required. Though the punishment was several times repeated and I was reduced to the most deplorable condition, I remained inflexible' (Rousseau 1953: 29). For Rousseau this injustice and cruelty marks the end of innocence, 'the earthly paradise' he had enjoyed till then; a gap now opens up between himself and others; he no longer looks on his elders as 'gods who read our hearts' (p.30). Yet this seemingly paradigmatic story of innocence and vulnerability being damaged by the harshness and cruelty of others is oddly duplicated by another anecdote. This time, Rousseau has indeed committed the crime he refuses to confess to: he has stolen a ribbon in order to give it to a pretty maidservant, Marion, when he has been employed as a valet by the Countess de Vercellis. When the ribbon is found on him, he defends himself by accusing Marion of having given it to him. They are both dismissed. In retrospect, Rousseau becomes his own accuser: 'I may have ruined a nice, honest, and decent girl, who was certainly worth a great deal more than I, and doomed her to disgrace and misery' (p.86). Indeed his remorse and need to confess this 'offence' have been so great that they are one of the chief motives for writing his *Confessions*: 'The burden, therefore, has rested till this day on my conscience without any relief; and I can affirm that the desire to some extent to rid myself of it has greatly contributed to my resolution of writing these *Confessions*' (p.88).

Paul de Man has offered a complex reading of this particular episode and in the process made an important distinction, which he believes also holds true for all autobiographical writing, between its 'cognitive' and 'performative' aspects, between what it means and what it does. Rousseau in effect does not limit himself simply to *telling* us about his crime, he also *excuses* it by reference to his contradictory inner feelings: 'But I should not fulfil the aim of this book if I did not at the same time reveal my inner feelings and hesitated to put up such excuses for myself as I honestly could' (Rousseau 1953: 88). However, whereas there is factual evidence of the theft – a ribbon was in fact stolen – we must, as Paul de Man suggests, simply take Rousseau's word for his feelings; there is no other available proof (de Man 1979a: 280). The performative dimension of the confession – the excuse – functions, then, in a different mode to the cognitive, as a verbal utterance which cannot be verified and which also keeps the meaning of the action he is confessing 'open'. The excuse fails to satisfy; it does not provide closure but could be both endlessly expanded and repeated (p.283).

Significantly, the feeling that Rousseau reveals in his attempt to excuse himself is shame: he has not meant to lie and implicate Marion, but has been overcome by shame when he was publicly exposed: 'My invincible sense of shame prevailed over everything. It was my shame that made me impudent, and the more wickedly I behaved the bolder my fear of confession made me' (Rousseau 1953: 88). Rousseau 'confesses' to the reader that his stealing of the ribbon had to do with his desire for Marion: the ribbon was intended as a gift to her. What de Man challenges is not the feeling of shame itself but where it is located. After all, why should Rousseau, either then or now, be ashamed to reveal a sexual desire which is neither transgressive nor forbidden? Instead what de Man suggests is that shame is intimately allied to exhibitionism and that there is a connection between hiding oneself and self-revelation. De Man believes that Marion herself is insignificant for Rousseau; she is, in effect, the signifier of a desire which belongs elsewhere. His shame is simply an 'excuse' for exposure, a 'ruse' which sanctions his confession (de Man 1979a: 286). His confession cannot make reparation to his victim; instead, according to de Man, Rousseau creates 'a stage on which to parade his disgrace' (p.28); he fulfils another desire, his real desire in writing, which is to compel public admiration for his inner self.

Following de Man's argument, a case could be made for there being less difference than first appeared between the incident with the comb and this later one with the ribbon: both involve the re-staging within writing of a scene of public exposure, where the performance of innocent feelings – or feelings of innocence – is also the real source of desire. Rousseau makes a drama out of his previously hidden emotions, justifying the interest and importance he, as auto-biographer, is claiming for himself. No wonder that Rousseau prefigured the comb episode with an account of the beatings administered by Mlle Lambercier and the erotic pleasure he derived from them. The persecutory role of other people in his life is one of Rousseau's recurrent themes. It is a role that confirms his shame and thus also, perversely, increases his pleasure; and it is because the pleasure is shameful and secret that it becomes all the more gratifying for him to reveal by confessing to it in his text.

The point de Man is making relates ultimately to autobiographical writing itself. The performative, according to de Man, will always be in excess of the cognitive dimension of autobiography. The textual 'I' seeks out excuses to perform itself; it creates dramas in order to stage the 'real' drama of the 'self'. What it clearly does not want to do is explain itself away through cognition. If everything could be understood, there would be nothing left to excuse and there would be no text, no justification or excuse for autobiography. For de Man the text, paradoxically, generates guilt in order to justify the excuse rather than the other way around; it is in search of an excuse for its own being (which it can never know), a reason for coming into existence at all. The point therefore is not *what* Rousseau confesses but the act of confession, the drama of the self.

In the *Confessions*, Rousseau presents himself as a shy man who is inhibited in his relationships with others from revealing his 'true nature'. He writes in order to achieve that self-possession which always eluded him in company. The nearest he can come to his ideal of spontaneous expression is reading his own work in public. The text becomes the writer's surrogate. On one occasion this stratagem proves an outstanding success. He decides to read from his novel *Julie* in order to 'save myself the embarrassment' of talking to Mme de Luxembourg, of whom he is in awe. Rousseau is rewarded with all the recognition he desires: 'Mme de Luxembourg was crazy about *Julie* and its author. She talked of nothing but me' (Rousseau 1953: 484). However, he receives a very different response to a public performance of the *Confessions* later on when his reading is greeted by indecipherable silence. This is the last paragraph of the *Confessions* and it is positioned as an 'afterword', outside the narrative:

> Thus I concluded my reading, and everyone was silent. Mme d'Egmont was the only person who seemed moved. She trembled visibly but quickly controlled herself, and remained quiet, as did the rest of the company. Such was the advantage I derived from my reading and my declaration.
>
> (Rousseau 1953: 606)

The slight bodily *frisson* quickly fades into the silent self-control shown by the rest of the audience who, in this act of physical withdrawal or sublimation, seem to prefigure later silent readers of Rousseau's text.

Rousseau, according to Jacques Derrida in another influential poststructuralist reading, uses writing as a 'supplement', a term which Rousseau also applies to the 'unnatural' act of masturbation: 'Soon I . . . learned that dangerous means of cheating Nature, which leads in young men of my temperament to various kinds of excesses' (Rousseau 1953: 108); later he also describes himself as 'seduced by this fatal advantage' (p.109). To describe writing as a supplement is to suggest that it is added on to speech; that it comes later, as supplementary. For Rousseau speaking has a 'naturalness' and immediacy which writing tries to imitate through a kind of 'artful ruse'; its artificiality attempts to 'be' natural; in other words, to 'cheat nature'. However, as Derrida points out, Rousseau is here describing a Utopian version of what it means to speak, 'speech as it should be or *should have been*' (p.141), rather than as it is. What Rousseau demonstrates in his autobiography, according to Derrida, is that it is up to writing to replace a deficiency or fill an absence where speaking should have been; it offers vicarious compensation to Rousseau who time and again fails to speak or to manage to make himself present through speaking. Writing thus takes the place of, or substitutes for, what is already lacking: 'If it represents and makes an image, it is by the anterior default of a presence' (p.145). The meaning of supplement as 'surplus', for Derrida, therefore, cannot be separated from its other meaning as 'substitute', and Rousseau's writing can be seen to circulate between them. The onanistic pleasure of writing is that it is both 'symbolic and immediate' (p.153); it defers but does not seem to; it satisfies what, without symbolic substitution, would never have been. Derrida's point is not just that we only have access to Rousseau's essential reality within the text but that there is no 'reality': there has never been anything but writing; there have only been 'supplements, subsitutive significations'. The idea of 'Nature' which Rousseau uses to name an originating source of meaning preceding the text has, according to Derrida, always already escaped; indeed it has never existed (p.159).The poststructuralist Rousseau, therefore, is almost the inverse of the Romantic one, for what this interpretation sees is that autobiography begins from the 'fatal advantage' of a writing which can only produce the 'mirage of the thing itself' (p.157) by means of a subsitutive process. In the silence which is all the 'advantage', as Rousseau says, he gains at the end of the *Confessions*, he is dispossessed *of* words but he is also dispossessed *by* words. He has become the author who is no longer recognized as the producer of his text.

The dilemma of Romantic autobiography, for which Rousseau seems to have provided such extensive exemplary material, lies in the way the notion of an original and authentic self, the transparency which for Rousseau was his 'natural' condition, is both presumed and put into question by representation itself, by a language which performs more than it means to, which does not correspond to experience, but introduces through displacement and excess other, unpredictable meanings. The Romantic autobiographer proclaims his originality but is also obsessed by a search for origins, for the absent 'maternal' or material ground of his being. To recover it, however, would also be to lose himself, and it is only because of the absence of origins that the narrative of their recovery – the autobiographical narrative – can be staged. According to Geoffrey Hartman's influential reading, the great paradox of Romanticism was that the vaunted 'return to nature', or the desire to overcome self-consciousness, could only be undertaken through consciousness itself. Wordsworth's *Prelude* begins with a longing for a subject that eludes him. In terms of Hartman's Romantic paradox, 'Wordsworth cannnot find his theme because he already has it: himself' (Hartman, in Chase 1993: 46, 49). Autobiography, in this sense, could be said to represent a privileged form for the Romantic writer as well as confirming his plight, the perplexity of a self forever recasting and repeating itself as text.

William Wordsworth began writing his long autobiographical poem, *The Prelude*, in which he intended to chart the growth of his own mind, in 1799, addressing it to his friend and mentor, Samuel Taylor Coleridge. Though completed in 1805, Wordsworth felt dissatisfied with it, and would go on 'retouching and revising' it for the rest of his life (de Selincourt 1932: xvii). The version published posthumously in 1850 is generally agreed to be inferior to the earlier one; yet it is also interesting to think about how the poem, in the very process of its production, remains indeterminate, in pursuit of an inviolable origin which inevitably gets dispersed into various different revised or substituted versions. The poet uses memory to attempt to return to the sources of his own poetic power in childhood, sadly diminished with the onset of maturity and the ascendancy of rationality over imagination. The poem becomes a means of restoring what has been lost, but the story of this restoration cannot be told as it never exists as a story in terms of a single narrative trajectory; rather Wordsworth remembers a series of past experiences out of chronological order, 'spots of time' (Wordsworth 1805: XI, 258) which revivify his writing in the present: 'Such moments worthy of all gratitude, / Are scatter'd everywhere' (Book XI, 274–5). The poem observes a gap between the poet's past and present selves, a 'Vacancy between me and those days' which can make him seem 'Two consciousnesses, conscious of myself / And of some other Being' (Book II, 32–3). However, the journey back to 'wholeness' can only be undertaken within the poem itself by the past being recomposed within the present time of writing. The 'vacancy' which the poem attempts to traverse is a space for the imagination but, as Paul Jay points out, the corollary of this is a dizzying self-consciousness (Jay 1984: 57). The poem could be read not as a quest for a beginning but as a series of interruptions which attempt to bring the poem back to its subject, which is none other than the poet himself.

The debate about whether Wordsworth had read Rousseau's *Confessions* or had been influenced by them is a complex one.

Nevertheless, these two autobiographical texts undoubtedly share some important features, drawing on 'a common psychological vocabulary of sensation, feeling, memory, and imagination' (Mitchell 1990: 646–7). Both texts reveal a reverence for Nature, a love of solitude and the attempt to recover childhood experience; in both, according to poststructuralist critics, the self-aware self is radically divided, endlessly and paradoxically repeating its self-division in the rhetoric of a unique, unified or pre-existing self. Nevertheless, Mitchell is right to point to important differences: Rousseau's outlook is more tragic, his view of human relations hopeless and embittered; Wordsworth goes on affirming the value of love, not least by invoking his friendship with Coleridge in the very address of the poem, but it is in their opposed treatments of guilt that the most interesting comparison can be made. As Mitchell suggests, 'Rousseau confesses everything and feels guilty for nothing', while 'Wordsworth confesses nothing and yet seems to feel excessive, unmotivated guilt for some unnamed crime' (p. 647).

From this point of view it is worth examining the famous boy-hood episode in *The Prelude* when Wordsworth steals a boat. At this moment, cast off from the shore, engaged in his 'act of stealth / And troubled pleasure', the child is pursued by his own guilty imaginings, the censorious adult projected on to the landscape itself:

> a huge Cliff,
> As if with voluntary power instinct,
> Uprear'd its head. I struck, and struck again,
> And, growing still in stature, the huge Cliff
> Rose up between me and the stars, and still,
> With measur'd motion, like a living thing,
> Strode after me.
>
> (Book I, 406–12)

The guilt is excessive, going far beyond what an adult might think 'reasonable', and the child's subjectivity can only be approached by

opening up a gap in interpretation: 'for many days my brain / Work'd
with a dim and undetermin'd sense / of unknown modes of being'
(418–20). The absence of 'determined' meaning could well indicate
repression, and the sexual nature of that repression might well be
read, or read into, the 'strokes' of the boat which the child 'rose upon',
which then returns as a vision of a potentized and frightening
(castrating?) landscape. However, the fearful presence which invades
the child's solitude, which takes on all the force of a gaze, is also a
kind of absence: 'There was a darkness, call it solitude, / Or blank
desertion, no familiar shapes / Of hourly objects, images of trees, / Of
sea or sky, no colours of green fields' (421–4). The traumatic memory
of a landscape which overwhelms the child with terror, which presents
itself as 'spectacle' rather than meaning, and leads to near extinction,
blanking his mind with 'huge and mighty Forms that do not live /
Like living men' (425–6), seems also to contain an intimation of
mortality, his future death. As we have seen, according to Paul de
Man, *The Prelude* (like all autobiography) is also a form of epitaph (de
Man 1993: 63; see Introduction: 14–15 of this volume): it is the
survival of writing beyond the grave, in which death, by writing, is
both anticipated and repressed. The poem reflects on a death which
is unimaginable; it also denies the death which has already happened
by presenting us with a vision, a writing which conceals its own status
as writing by, quite literally, returning it as a face or a gaze. While
Rousseau's guilt helps to generate the text in the endless play of self-
justifying excuses, Wordsworth's assures him of a haunting and
inexplicable indeterminacy of affect – a spectral presence – which
attempts to evade the lifeless finality of the text itself.

Wordsworth's autobiography is also, of course, a poem, and,
because of this obvious difference, may be seen as able to assume,
unlike Rousseau's *Confessions*, a set of values which supersede his
material condition, which are indeed transcendent or sublime,
too vast for the rational mind to comprehend. When Wordsworth
finds himself in the presence of Nature, it is also the occasion for
seeing his imagination's own spaciousness and sublimity. This is

never more the case than in the famous crossing of the Alps in Book VI when Wordsworth offers a paean of praise to the Imagination: 'Imagination! lifting up itself / Before the eye and progress of my Song / Like an unfather'd vapour; here that Power, / In all the might of its endowments, came / Athwart me' (525–9). However, the problem with this passage, and its exulted sense of imaginative potency, is that it also diverts attention from a failure, an anticlimactic crossing of the Alps which has happened to the poet almost unawares. The culminating scene of Alpine grandeur could be said to repeat others where Nature in its sublime aspect is almost too much to bear, overwhelming the poet with a possible loss of self. It is perhaps providential that Wordsworth misses the supreme moment, since, instead of simply being defeated, he is able to recapture it in words and represent the processes of his own subjectivity. However, the climb down from the peaks, which is also a descent into words, paradoxically involves the poet in the evocation of a Divine face, the finding of a 'presence' which exceeds the poet's own:

> Tumult and peace, the darkness and the light
> Were all like workings of one mind, the features
> Of the same face, blossoms upon one tree,
> Characters of the great Apocalypse.

> (567–570)

The poet turns from a missed encounter with sublimity only to find himself face to face with the Divine, and its apocalyptic and unreadable inscription. If sublimity threatens the self, perhaps even more threatening is the discovery that writing which does not lift itself into ephemeral and mystical realms may succumb to its own inert nature. The attempt to meet sublimity on its own terms, even if such an attempt is doomed to failure, is also a way of trying to guarantee the existence of a subject beyond the text. In Mary Jacobus' interpretation of this passage, the Divine signs are a privileged and compensatory writing, protecting against the even greater anticlimax of the literal text: 'writing comes in aid of writing, reanimating the dead page with intimations of a meaning that always exceeds it' (Jacobus 1989: 15). The Wordsworthian autobiographer needs the sublime, we could say, in order to give life to himself in a Divine form, beyond the deathly finality of the book. The sublime could be said to be what offsets the anxieties called up by the very act of turning himself into (lifeless) words.

Gayatri Spivak has suggested that Romantic autobiography, with its emphasis on the singular 'I', was premised on the repression of sexual difference (Spivak 1987: 76). The transcendent subject, as we have seen, sustains its unity with difficulty, positioning himself beyond the body as pure consciousness, risking the recognition of his own self-alienation within language. For Wordsworth the female – be it Nature or the mother – is what the heroically questing self must separate himself from, at the same time opening up a thereby unassuageable desire for a return to a maternal source or origin. Women, insofar as they appear in *The Prelude* at all, are located in the realm of the pre-sexual, and assimilated to the masculine self, the threat of otherness thus subsumed: Dorothy Wordsworth is significantly apostrophized as 'Child of my Parents! Sister of my Soul!' (Book XIII, 204); or they are cast out, as in the episode of the prostitute in Book VII, whose solicitations are invoked only to be denied and who is thus forced to carry the whole burden of sexuality herself. Wordsworth is notably silent in *The Prelude* about his own illegitimate child. Yet sexual difference cannot be wholly repressed; it returns in the unstable rhetoric of gender which pervades the poem and which Wordsworth struggles to control. As Anne Mellor has argued, at the end of *The Prelude*, the imagination through which Wordsworth has sought to prove his autonomous masculine identity against a feminine Nature, having tracked *her* 'up *her* way sublime' (Book XIII, 282; my emphasis), reveals its residual femininity (Mellor 1993: 151). Difference installs itself at the heart of the poetic subject, and both the autonomous self and its masculine identification are open to question once again.

Romantic selfhood, based on notions of the organic development of the implicitly masculine subject, also requires the strenuous repression of its Others. Perhaps it is not surprising, therefore, as Barbara Johnson has argued, that the most powerful story told by a woman in the Romantic period should be about a deviant creation or monster (Johnson 1987: 145). Mary Shelley's *Frankenstein* (1818) is not of course an autobiography but a fiction; moreover it is a fiction which is transmitted through the first-person accounts of three men. Yet Frankenstein's monster, with all his poignant emotions of yearning and unfulfilment, not to mention his fragmented body pieced together into the semblance of wholeness, could be read as a perverse figure for autobiography, for what it means to create a life in one's own image. If Shelley hides her transgressive act of female authorship behind the personae of articulate men while casting her women into the role of passive victims, traces of her struggle to produce the 'hideous progeny' of her book are incorporated into her text, becoming the raw material which is taken over by Frankenstein in his own desperate act of creation. Shelley turns away from autobiography, from the impossibility of fashioning a life on the model of men, only for the monstrousness of the desire to assume a life of its own in her text. Clearly we are not far away from the subject of the next chapter and Freud's understanding of the repressed as the uncanny or *unheimlich* which can strangely pre-empt the familiar, producing ghosts and terrifying doubles.

Whatever doubts are raised in relation to the notion of Romantic selfhood, however, its assumptions have continued to exert an important influence on the writing and understanding of autobiography. Paradoxically, as we shall see in the next chapter, the notion of the natural, Romantic self outlives the recognition of its own impossibility, called back to life again as a nostalgic revenant or, with a wary realism, invoked as a necessary strategy on a route to somewhere else.

2

SUBJECTIVITY, REPRESENTATION AND NARRATIVE

FREUD'S UNCONSCIOUS

This chapter is primarily concerned with three twentieth-century theorists and practitioners of autobiography: Sigmund Freud, Roland Barthes and Jacques Derrida, whose writings, chronologically, succeed the autobiographies analysed in the previous chapter. However, their work has already, to some degree, been anticipated. This is because, in attempting to survey a historical tradition of autobiographical writing, however sketchily, it is important to take account of how that tradition has been formed by certain key assumptions which are also open to question. The modern disillusionment with the unitary subject does not simply create a break, opening up a new critical perspective; it also casts a backward shadow, transforming how we read previous writing. As Candace Lang argues, 'not only is autobiography "in the Augustinian sense" no longer possible, *it never was*' (Lang 1982: 5). It is not that a unified self was once available and can be rediscovered in past auto-biographies; there is a sense in which it always was a historical and ideological construct, an effect of discourse.

This notion that the present can retroactively alter the past could be seen as one of Sigmund Freud's major insights. Freud characteristically looked to the past for explanations: it was the past, imperfectly located as past, which created the neurotic symptom; and it was the childhood drama of love, hate and jealousy in relation to one's parents – the Oedipus complex – which set the scene for the adult's later affective life. In treating history as developmental or evolutionary, a process with a beginning and an implied goal or telos, Freud could be seen as the inheritor of the great explanatory narratives of the nineteenth century. The past creates the foundation for the present and future and illuminates the flaws and diversions as well as the normal pattern for individual growth. Yet childhood and neurotic symptoms, according to Freud, also belonged to the adult's prehistory, a distant region which remained repressed or unconscious and which thus existed outside the normal processes of time and history. The past in this sense can enter the present only as repetition or intrusive memory, disrupting linearity and giving rise to a more complex temporality. To remember is not to restore something previously lost, to find a link in a chain which was previously missing. Rather the past can only be known belatedly, restructuring in the present what had previously been thought of as past. The past, then, lying dormant or latent within the subject, seems to come from outside their lived experience as a momentous and violent shock, causing them retrospectively to recast their sense of themselves and the life they have led. History is never definitive or finally known, therefore, but is capable of constant alteration as more is remembered or released into consciousness, causing the subject to think both the past and the present differently.

Freud's thinking on the relation between narrative and the subject has important consequences for the understanding of autobiography and how we remember our lives. In effect it is possible to ally him with two conflicting notions of time and narrative order, and it is the difference between them that we need to understand here. As a theorist and scientist he developed explanatory accounts of the workings of the human psyche which relied on concepts of both origins and goals; as a student of the unconscious he was aware of highly complex connections between desires and memories which obeyed no 'rational' system but required the careful following of the individual subject's own 'unconscious' associative links. In the four extended case histories which Freud published between 1894 and 1918, and which we could also read as experiments in life-writing, what becomes apparent is that he cannot maintain his scientific stance; indeed his subject keeps escaping his own presumption of mastery. From his very first attempt to write a case history in 1894, Freud was disturbed by his inability to draw a clear division between the scientific and the literary:

> It still strikes me myself as strange that the case histories I write should read like short stories and that, as one might say, they lack the serious stamp of science. I must console myself with the reflection that the nature of the subject is evidently responsible for this, rather than any preference of my own.
>
> (Freud 1974: 231)

Freud becomes a novelist, or at least a short story writer, despite himself, and a short story writer, we may add, of a particularly modernist bent. In order to tell his patient's story and interpret it, Freud is forced to tell a story of his own, one which necessarily implicates him as narrator/author. If the theory is that the patient should in the end come into possession of their own story, what the case histories demonstrate is a more ambiguous and inconclusive dialogue between the patient's version and Freud's own.

In his study of the 'Wolf Man' (1918), Freud acknowledged the impossibility of the task he has set himself of unifying within one narrative the different temporal layers which belonged to the patient's story and his own interpretation:

> I am unable to give either a purely historical or a thematic account of my patient's story; I can write a history neither of the treatment nor of the illness, but I shall find myself obliged to combine the two methods of presentation.
>
> (Freud 1979a: 240)

The case study hinges on the notion of retroaction: Freud's hypothesis was that the Wolf Man witnessed his parents having intercourse when he was 18 months old but that the shock of that impression was deferred until he had attained some sexual understanding of what he had seen. Freud is forced to follow a similarly confusing chronology: 'We must here break off the discussion of his sexual development until new light is thrown from the later stages of his history upon these earlier ones' (Freud 1979a: 280). The problem for Freud is that such early scenes are not necessarily to be differentiated from phantasies with which they will have become entangled: they require to be 'divined – constructed – gradually and laboriously from an aggregate of indications' (p.285). The difficulties of analysis reproduce the difficulties of the patient; Freud is also implicated in 'constructing' fictions in his attempt to interpret his patient's history.

In his most famous case history, that of 'Dora' (1905), Freud is forced to complete the story on his own, Dora having peremptorily walked out on the analysis. Freud was disconcerted by the 'frag-mentary' nature of the case history which seemed to indict his own capacity for coherent thought. Freud must 'restore what is missing' himself, again offering his own constructions for what is unavailable or 'mutilated' within the patient's material (Freud 1977: 41). Despite the fact, which he acknowledges, that any neurosis will to a degree remain bewildering, even to the most practised analyst, he still finds it difficult to suspend his own yearning for closure: 'If the work had been continued, we should no doubt have obtained the fullest

possible enlightenment upon every particular of the case' (p.40). Yet
what becomes evident is not so much what is missing from the
case history as what Freud must himself exclude. Freud marginalizes
the conflicting evidence – Dora's attachment to her mother, her
homosexual attraction to Frau K. – in order to demonstrate Dora's
'hysterical' resistance to 'normal' heterosexuality. For later commentators on 'Dora', what appears troubling is the meaning of femininity
which Freud can only 'know' in terms of his own Oedipal story, and
therefore in a fragmentary or incomplete way. In other words, what
is at stake here is not just Dora's unconscious but Freud's: his desire
is to contain the threat which Dora poses to his definition of
femininity and thus to his potency as a (male) scientist as well.

Freud was aware that his theory of the unconscious and its
workings was always in danger of being 'watered down' (Freud 1935:
95), its new and disturbing form of knowledge diluted, even though
he, himself, was often at odds with the implications of his own
theory in his desire to claim mastery over it. The challenge of Freud's
later interpreter, Jacques Lacan, from the 1920s onwards is not
that he 'revised' Freudian theory or added to it, but that he drew
out its radical and disruptive potential. Lacan recognized that the
Freudian unconscious was at odds with the traditions of humanism
which Freud inherited and within which he tried to situate himself.
Whereas Freud's ultimate aim was to restore meaning by providing
a therapeutic cure, Lacan drew attention to the status of the unconscious as a gap or a lost moment. For Lacan there was no way of
'knowing' the unconscious, since it cannot be circumscribed in any
temporal structure. Instead it appears in a moment of intuition
which disappears again before any conclusion can be reached (Lacan
1979: 32). Claims to mastery founder on an irreconcilable split
within the subject; the unconscious forever escapes the subject who
presumes to know, but who is, unknown to himself, mired in misapprehension and delusion. When Lacan stated that 'the unconscious
is structured like a language' (p.20) he was not only bringing his
own post-Freudian understanding of linguistics into play, he was

also drawing attention to the only form in which the unconscious ever makes itself available. 'The analyst's interpretation merely reflects the fact that the unconscious, if it is what I say it is, namely, a play of the signifier, has already in its formations – dreams, slips of the tongue or pen, witticisms or symptoms – proceeded by interpretation' (Lacan 1979: 130). Psychoanalysis shares the same fate as the subject: it starts in the labyrinth of language from which it can never expect to escape; the unconscious presents itself in terms of the allusive effects of language which can only be interpreted again by the analyst within language. As therapy, psychoanalysis is always concerned with the spoken word both as the analytic material and as the only means the analyst has of interpreting it. There is no way out of the twists and turns of language (Bowie 1991: 48).The subject is constituted within a (foreign) language which speaks him. Whereas Freud was anxious about the complicity of psychoanalysis with literature, Lacan finds within literature the 'seeds' and confirmation of an intricate and multi-layered language, which speaks more than it knows.

For Lacan, the implication of Freudian theory was that the subject was never more than a fantasy of a unified subject, already inhabited by 'the Other'. Lacan uses the term 'the Other' to designate both the 'otherness' of the unconscious and the other to whom the subject directs his speech and who is thus the locus of meaning and identification. For Lacan what he famously designated the 'mirror stage' was the founding moment for the subject and the structure through which the subject assumes his identity, as the unified image that is reflected back to him from outside, from the place of the Other. Traditional notions of the mirror were that it returned a more or less faithful likeness of an original, pre-existing self. Lacan argued that the mirror constructs the self, that what is 'known' as the self is the cohesiveness of a reflection which the subject fantasizes as real. Clearly this also has implications for autobiography which has often employed the idea of the mirror as an analogy for the self-reflective project of autobiographical writing. Read in the light of

Lacan's mirror stage, autobiography, according to Shari Benstock, 'reveals the impossibility of its own dream: what begins in the presumption of self-knowledge ends in the creation of a fiction that covers over the premises of its construction'. The subject, through autobiography, strives towards the 'false symmetry' of the mirror, a unified self which can only ever be a fiction (Benstock 1988: 11, 12).

The 'return to Freud' inaugurated by Lacan recognized that no knowledge existed outside the destabilizing effect of the unconscious and that the interpretive procedures that Freud initiated could be equally applied to his own texts. Returning to Freud was not to invoke his presence as final authority but to put into play all that was unfinished about his texts, all that was Other about them or at odds with their presumed meaning. Applying this to Freud's own autobiographical text, *An Autobiographical Study* (1935), means, therefore, that the most Freudian thing about it could be less what it tells us about Freud than what it does not. If we read it from a post-Lacanian perspective, it becomes, perhaps, a form of desire in relation to autobiography; an autobiography through which 'Freud' returns as the inexplicable haunting his own text, as the space, the interval between one self and an Other.

Freud in fact wrote his *An Autobiographical Study* in 1924, ten years earlier than the above publication date, in response to a request from a German editor who wished to compile a collection of short studies by members of the medical profession which would thus illuminate current medical knowledge. As Freud's translator, James Strachey, suggests, 'the stress was thus laid by implication on the professional rather than the personal histories' (Freud 1935: 9) and it would therefore be easy to interpret how Freud presented himself as determined by the aims of the collection itself. However, this particular emphasis seems to have suited Freud's own 'autobiographical urge'. In the later postscript to the *Study* he himself chooses to 'justify' his life in terms of a triumphant sacrifice of the personal to science:

> *The Autobiographical Study* shows how psychoanalysis came to
> be the whole content of my life and rightly assumes that no per-
> sonal experiences of mine are of any interest in comparison to
> my relations to that science.
>
> (Freud 1935: 131)

Oddly, then, for someone uniquely aware of the decisive influence
of the hidden aspects of the psyche on the public self, Freud pushes
his own private and affective life to the margins of his autobiographical text. The only relations that matter are, as Freud says,
the relations with science. His mother receives no mention at all;
his father fleetingly enters the text but only to be the servant of
Freud's autonomy and professional independence: 'Though we lived
in very limited circumstances, my father insisted that, in my choice
of profession, I should follow my own inclination' (Freud 1935: 13).
His fiancée is presented as a hindrance to his work and the reason
he did not achieve fame at an earlier age, though he denies – with
rather obvious unconscious meaning – that he bears her 'any grudge'
(p.25). His friendship with Breuer is a price that he painfully
but 'inescapably' has to pay for the development of psychoanalysis
(p.33). This disavowal of dependency at an emotional level extends
to Freud's intellectual sources and influences as well. Though he
admits to having learned from others, notably Breuer and Charcot,
he also believed he alone understood the wider significance of their
ideas. He deliberately avoided reading the work of the philosophers
Arthur Schopenhauer and Friedrich Nietzsche, whose work was in
some ways close to his own, until late in life. If psychoanalysis could
be said to originate with Freud, psychoanalysis also proved his
originality: 'I stood alone and had to do all the work myself', Freud
writes of the important formative phase (p.101).

It could be argued that one of the desires that is encoded by
autobiography, and which Freud's *Study* seems to exemplify, is that
of becoming, within the realm of the symbolic, one's own progenitor,

of assuming authorship of one's own life. This has a clear echo within Freud's psychoanalytic thinking. In one of his most famous formulations, his theory of the Oedipus/Castration complex, the female genitals remain 'undiscovered'. As he writes in the *Study*: 'Only the male genitals play a part in it, and the female ones remain undiscovered' (Freud 1935: 67); the female genitals exist as the opaque reality which Freud's theory must convert into a symbolic lack or absence in order clearly to maintain its own unity and coherence as theory. As we have already seen in relation to Freud's case study of 'Dora', the male within Freud's theory of sexuality becomes the theoretical model for the female, while the female – fragmentary and incomplete – is made theoretically impotent, denied the possibility of a different theory of her own. However, the 'undiscovered female genitals' could also be said to function in another way: undiscovered in the sense that Freud himself described the pre-Oedipal lying beneath the Oedipal; like a yet to be explored archaeological site, they contain a repressed or forgotten knowledge of the conception and birth that necessarily preceded his own self-conception within language. By emphasizing his originality and the close correspondence between his life and his intellectual achievement, Freud could be said to have attempted to exclude the mother or feminine Other whose identity threatens his own.

As we have already noted, Lacan suggested that psychoanalysis itself may be at odds with the kind of singularity and transcendence that Freud is proposing within his autobiography; on the contrary, Lacan argued that psychoanalysis calls into question the possibility of a 'subject who knows' by positing its inevitable relation with the unknowable Other. Freud himself had written in 1910 that as a psychoanalyst 'one may sometimes make a wrong surmise, and one is never in a position to discover the whole truth' (Freud 1979b: 221–2). The very obvious 'wrong surmise' that Freud makes in his *Study* is that he would die soon after he completed it in 1925; instead he was still alive to add a postscript some ten years later. The text that we have therefore offers a rewriting of the ending, revealing the error of his first more tragic perception of finality from the perspective of his unexpected survival. Death, as if we had been transposed from a Greek tragedy to a Shakespearean comedy, is no longer the inevitable end, and authoritative utterance, such as Freud assumes in the *Study*, loses its meaning. Indeed in the postscript Freud is ambivalently positioned between being the author of cultural and historical studies which have taken his writing in ambitious new directions, and the thinker he was before, who has added nothing original to his own theory of psychoanalysis. Freud in a sense and, despite his efforts, cannot regain mastery of the difference he makes to his previous text. His autobiography exceeds its own conclusion(s) and he can only recover himself through splitting and repetition; there is always more than one interpretation to be accounted for. In a fascinatingly brief disclaimer towards the end of the postscript he also opens up the possibility of reading other of his texts as autobiographical or of recognizing that there may be more than one text of the self:

> And here I may be allowed to break off these autobiographical notes. The public has no claim to learn any more of my personal affairs – of my struggles, my disappointments, and my successes. I have in any case been more open and frank in some of my writings (such as *The Interpretation of Dreams* and *The Psychoanalysis of Everyday Life*) than people usually are who describe their lives for their contemporaries or for posterity. I have had small thanks for it and from my experience I cannot recommend anyone to follow my example.
>
> (Freud 1935: 135)

Dreading disclosure which may, after all, have already happened and longing for recognition, Freud also surrenders the omnipotence he has claimed for himself throughout his *Study*. His denial of 'relations' makes a suitably Freudian return. In the transference which occurs between writer and reader, he can only imagine a reader who withholds recognition from him, from whom he receives small thanks, while also clearly desiring from his public some other, more gratifying relationship. According to Lacan, 'the Other latent or not, is even beforehand, present in the subjective revelation' (Lacan 1979: 130). Freud can neither dispose of the Other's implication within his own discourse, nor conceal the traces of what exceeds or precedes his own claim to mastery. Derrida, commenting in a suitably obscure way about Freud's attempts at autobiography through self-analysis, suggests the supreme paradox of Freud's thinking: Freud's self-knowledge is ultimately knowledge of what 'he', the subject, cannot know: 'He who called himself the first, and therefore the only, one to have attempted, if not to have defined it, did not himself know and this must be taken into account' (Derrida 1991: 532).

BARTHES' AUTOBIOGRAPHICAL SIGNS

Roland Barthes' autobiography *Roland Barthes by Roland Barthes* (1977) is probably the most famous attempt to write an autobiography 'against itself'. While purporting to be an autobiography, it deconstructs from within the major assumptions underlying the genre. The text's most salient break with tradition is achieved through discarding the first-person singular and substituting instead multiple-subject positionings: 'he', 'R.B.', 'you' and 'I' exchange places almost arbitrarily in an attempt to reinforce the effect of distance between the writer and the written text: 'I had no other solution than to *rewrite* myself – at a distance, a great distance – here and now. . . . Far from reaching the core of the matter, I remain on the surface' (p.142). For Barthes the essentialized subject, the subject whose depths are waiting to be revealed, is an illusion, an ideological construct to be resisted and displaced. As is appropriate for the writer who famously proclaimed in 1968 that the author is dead, his autobiographical subject can never authenticate his reality but only go on adding indefinitely to his many different spectral forms of identity:

This book is not a book of 'confessions'; not that it is insincere, but because we have a different knowledge today than yesterday; such knowledge can be summarized as follows: What I write about myself is never *the last word*: the more 'sincere' I am, the more interpretable I am, under the eye of other examples than those of the old authors, who believed they were required to submit themselves to but one law: *authenticity*.

(Barthes 1977: 120)

For Barthes, the subject can neither recapture the past, restoring it like a 'monument' (p.56), nor aim towards some ideal of transcendence in the future: there is no other place of radiant unification which can redeem the subject outside or behind the discourse in which he constructs and deconstructs himself. Barthes, therefore, with unmistakable ostentation, not only disperses the autobiographical subject between positions or pronouns, he also rigorously eschews narrative for the fragment, using the alphabet to ensure a random ordering of autobiographical snippets or self-reflections which deny the subject both origin and destiny:

The alphabetical order erases everything, banishes every origin. Perhaps in places, certain fragments seem to follow one another by some affinity; but the important thing is that these little networks not be connected, that they not slide into a single enormous network which would be the structure of the book, its meaning. It is in order to halt, to deflect, to divide this descent of discourse toward a destiny of the subject, that at certain moments the alphabet calls you to order (to disorder) and says: *Cut! Resume the story in another way*.

(Barthes 1977: 148)

The book then offers repeated beginnings; not the reconstruction of a past nor a writing about the past but the continuing accretion, through the present act of writing, of new layers that work to 'abolish' his 'previous truth' (p.56). It would be wrong, however, to see the past as simply excluded by Barthes; rather it is stripped of its ideological function as a privileged source of meaning, as the 'natural' ground of identity. What Barthes does is to resist the nostalgia which transfers desire to the past, which makes the past the locus of a longed-for but irretrievable unity. Instead he 'freewheels' in language, collapsing the distinction between the present and the past; he creates a 'patchwork' of discursive fragments without reference to the past or the present; both equally constitute the 'surface' of the text in the 'here and now'. By writing, he adds 'to the books, to the themes, to the memories, to the texts, another utterance, without my ever knowing whether it is about my past or my present that I am speaking' (p.142).

Psychoanalysis figures in Barthes' text as one of the discourses which informs but does not contain his own. He can 'make use' of psychoanalysis, he writes, only if he does not look at it directly (Barthes 1977: 153). Like all 'triumphant discourse' (p.47), psychoanalysis, when it is perceived as a body of knowledge or opinion or, in Barthes' term, *doxa*, excludes difference or excess. Barthes associates this difference with a relation to the living principle of writing – 'the Text of life, life-as-text' (p.64). It is interesting to note here that if autobiography is rejected by Barthes as a set of generic conventions already in existence, it is nevertheless recognized by him as a space of difference within discourse. The term which Barthes takes over from psychoanalysis is 'the Imaginary', a term originally used by Lacan to designate the repertoire of imaginary identifications and mirror images through which the subject covers his relations with the external world in order to ameliorate its otherness. Like Lacan, Barthes sees the subject as diffracted through a mirror, identified with his own delusional reflected gaze: 'what actually belongs to me is *my* image-repertoire, my phantasmatics' (pp.152–3). Much of *Barthes by Barthes* is involved with recognizing that a coherent self is a fiction, that it must always involve being seen from a distance, through the perspective of the Other. In one of the captions which accompany the photographs at the beginning of the book, Barthes writes: 'Where is your authentic body? You are the only one who can never see yourself except as an image' (p.152). Yet, through the *activity* of writing, he – or 'I' – is also on the inside, pleasurably surrounding himself with the words and images. Barthes can escape from the 'image-repertoire' in the space of work; words themselves, freed from their known place – their pigeon-holes – and attached to desire, can take the place of transitional objects. They can blossom and float, becoming valued objects of play or fantasy: 'As for the child, these favourite words constitute a part of his arena; and like transitional objects, they are of uncertain status' (p.130).

For Barthes the most important of such words is the 'body' (Barthes 1977: 130). It is a word which returns throughout the text and which Barthes frees from notions of the known, discrete, singularized body: '"Which body? We have several"' (p.60). The body precisely resists its own conceptualization (p.80). Missing from stereotypes (p.90), it is the body which creates difference, which inflects discourse by tracing within it its own movement of pleasure and desire: 'The body is the irreducible difference, and at the same time it is the principle of all structuration (since structuration is what is Unique in structure)' (p.175). The body creates a 'passion of meaning' (p.161), a disturbance or space where something happens to language, where the body's presence both animates and displaces meaning, makes meaning both mobile and irrecoverably somewhere else. For Barthes the most 'meaningful' discourse is discourse which does not allow itself to be 'caught', but which 'rustles' with different meanings, with a *frisson* or excitation which moves language away from definitive forms, from signs 'grimly weighted' by signifieds (p.98). Barthes' own 'most meaningful' language is marked by its entanglement with the body it also evokes, with an inspiration (movement or breath) which comes from the body: 'meaning, before collapsing into in-significance, shudders still . . . it remains fluid, shuddering with a faint ebullition' (pp.97–8).

The body also has a relation to 'theatre', the space for Barthes where all the divergent paths in his writing cross: 'At the crossroads of the entire *oeuvre*, perhaps the Theater' (Barthes 1977: 177). Barthes' conceptualization of theatre is Brechtian; that is, as for Brecht, the actor never simply identifies with the character he performs: 'I am speaking about myself in the manner of the Brechtian actor who must distance his character: "show" rather than incarnate him' (p.168). Barthes performs his 'imaginary' as if he were demonstrating or rehearsing different parts, distancing himself from them at the same time as scrutinizing them from different perspectives. To 'stage an image-system', as Barthes is doing in this book, means to arrange the perspectives, the roles and the limits; it is to give it a certain topology (p.105). The body in performance can belong to different scenes, without becoming merely a representation of the body; the body moving through different spaces and performing different roles is not fictitious; it is being used in a way which is both 'contingent' and 'essential' (p.183). It does not so much provide one location as many different ones, breaking up any simple identification, creating distance and multiple perspectives: 'The image-repertoire is taken over by several masks (*personae*), distributed according to the depth of the stage (and yet *no one – personne*, as we say in French – is behind them)' (p.120).

Yet however ironically or critically Barthes treats autobiography and the notion of the unitary subject which it has traditionally enshrined, he also undertakes his project within a form which still signifies to him as an autobiography. Sean Burke has argued that it is important to distinguish between critique and rejection: while Barthes puts the 'duplicities of representation' under pressure, making visible at every turn the impossibility of escape into an unmediated selfhood, he also resituates autobiography within a different critical moment. Autobiography survives its reconfiguring by poststructuralism, by absorbing and acknowledging self-critique. According to Sean Burke, 'to see the demise of autobiography in Roland Barthes is quite simply to affirm a greatly simplified conception of the autobiographical act . . . as though when a genre or mode of writing advertises its inherent problematics it is thereby denying or destroying itself' (Burke 1992: 189).

That autobiography does survive, albeit in a different form, signals not just its resilience but also, as Barthes himself admits, the limits of his own deconstructive gestures towards it. To fragment the subject and expose its illusions of unity may be, as we have seen, an ideological imperative for Barthes; however, he also raises doubts about whether such a project can ever be totally achieved. In line with his many destabilizing gestures in *Roland Barthes*, Barthes is finally also sceptical of his own strategies of fragmentation:

> I have the illusion to suppose that by breaking up my discourse I cease to discourse in terms of the imaginary about myself, attenuating the risk of transcendence; but since the fragment (haiku, maxim, *pensée*, journal entry) is *finally* a rhetorical genre and since rhetoric is that layer of language which best presents itself to interpretation, by supposing I disperse myself I merely return, quite docilely, to the bed of the imaginary.
>
> (Barthes 1977: 95)

In order for Barthes' fragmented, disjointed discourse to be possible another scene must exist. The fragmented self-image – the body in bits and pieces, to use Lacanian terminology – can only, paradoxically, in the end be known and represented from the perspective of an imaginary wholeness. Fragmentation, cast in the form of a *rhetoric* of fragmentation, comes only after the mirror stage and the constitution of the subject through the illusory recognition of unity, even though it attempts to represent what came before. What appears, therefore, to disperse the unified subject is simply a further projection of it; the violent shattering of a unified identity leads back 'docilely' to the primary identification of the subject in the imaginary. It is still the case, of course, that the mirror stage produces only an illusion of identity, an imaginary wholeness, but both past and future representations of the self are necessarily rooted in it. There is no way back through the mirror; nothing, or no one, exists on the other side.

Barthes' last book, *Camera Lucida* (1984), was published some five years after his experimental, ludic autobiography. Ostensibly about photography, it also returns to the problems of the autobiographical but with a sense of urgency and almost overwhelming pain. Written in the immediate aftermath of his mother's death, the book's quest to discover what photography is 'in itself' (Barthes 1984: 3) merges with another quest: the autobiographical quest for the 'essence' of the beloved person which no image can ever quite seem to give back to him (p.107). Photographs had also featured in *Barthes by Barthes* as a privileged site of the author's pleasure and fascination which he had positioned in the book before the text and without pagination, just as psychologically the 'image-repertoire' could be said to precede, or be outside, writing. 'The image-repertoire will therefore be closed at the onset of productive life. . . . Another repertoire will then be constituted: that of writing.' In *Camera Lucida*, therefore, photography returns as a different kind of representational space where questions of essence, which are treated as fallacious within writing where meaning is always plural and substitutive, can again be raised. In *Camera Lucida* Barthes goes on to develop his famous theory of the *punctum*, the word he coins to describe a piercing, uncodifiable detail that can pass from photograph to viewer and which is powerful enough to connect the spectator again with the 'real' of the past. By the 'real', Barthes means, like Lacan, an essence which is unsymbolizable, but where he differs from Lacan is in conceiving of situations where the threshold to the real can be crossed. According to Barthes, the photograph can offer such an opportunity; it can succeed where texts cannot in offering 'the unheard-of identification of reality ("*that has been*") with truth ("there-she-is!"): it becomes both evidential and exclamative' (p.113); through its appeal to 'the absolute particular' (p.4), it can communicate what cannot be put into words.

Barthes' fascination with photographs could be seen, as Rick Rylance suggests, in terms of a surprisingly naive denial of the range and sophistication of photographic trickery (Rylance 1994: 132). However, in the access that photographs at least *seem* to offer him to the 'real', his turning to photography also indicates a dissatisfaction with the 'reductiveness' of writing (Barthes 1984: 8), a kind of humanist residue that was also perhaps evident in *Barthes by Barthes*, in the paradoxical 'return' of the 'wholeness' which his text also continually dismisses and transgresses. 'Totality' is the question, quite literally, which *Barthes by Barthes* comes back to in the end (Barthes 1977: 180).

In *Camera Lucida* all photographs lead to one photograph: Barthes' quest for the meaning of photography leads him as if back to the beginning, to a photograph of his mother, which uniquely among his photographs of her seems to reveal 'the truth of the face I had loved' (Barthes 1984: 67). Strangely, however, this photograph is not a photograph of his mother as he ever could have known her. It is not a photograph taken during their life together. Instead it is a picture of her, aged 5, posing with her brother outside a Winter Garden. 'I studied the little girl and at last rediscovered my mother' (p.69), Barthes writes. The 'initiatic path' that has taken him to the moment of this discovery has also taken him to 'the end of all language', a recognition of the unique being of his mother 'in which words fail': 'the rare, perhaps unique evidence of the "So, yes, so much and no more"' (p.109). Though Barthes derives a theory of photography from this one photograph, 'the only photograph which assuredly existed for me', it also remains private, hidden from the eyes of the reader. 'It exists only for me', he states uncompromisingly. The book leads back to the space of the personal, which is also an unrepresented space that exists outside or beyond the text.

For Barthes this space is also presented as a feminine or maternal space. If in *Camera Lucida* the death of the mother occasions the search for an authentic photograph of her, and an enquiry into what is authentic about photographs, it also seems to require an autobiographical return to the intimacy of her dying. As in the photograph, mother and son have here changed places, with the mother occupying the place of the child and Barthes offering maternal sustenance:

> During her illness, I nursed her, held the bowl of tea she liked because it was easier to drink from than from a cup; she had become my little girl, uniting for me with that essential child she was in her first photograph. In Brecht, by a reversal I used to admire a great deal, it is the son who (politically) educates the mother; yet I never educated my mother, never converted her to anything at all; in a sense I never 'spoke' to her, never 'discoursed' in her presence, for her; we supposed, without saying anything of the kind to each other, that the frivolous insignificance of language, the suspension of images must be the very space of love, its music.
>
> (Barthes 1984: 72)

According to Barthes, the mother belongs to a place outside discourse, or at least outside the persuasiveness of theoretical discourse. Earlier we saw how Freud had implicitly positioned himself as theorist against the threat of the feminine or maternal body. For other theorists too, matricide becomes 'our vital necessity, the sine-qua-non condition of our individuation' (Kristeva 1989: 27–8); according to this view, the subject, by taking up their place within the symbolic, by entering language, in effect kills the mother, substituting words for her body which is forever lost. However, by identifying himself with his mother, Barthes also keeps her alive: 'ultimately I experienced her . . . as my feminine child' (Barthes 1984: 72). Her real dying replaces her symbolic murder. For Barthes it seems that the mother leads away from theory towards autobiography where, though her dying is represented, her death can be endlessly postponed. Drawn back into a mournful relationship with his mother Barthes writes autobiographically, but is there a necessary relationship between autobiography and the maternal? And what is the relation between the mother's real death and her symbolic murder? These are questions which Jacques Derrida also raises and which we will return to again.

DERRIDA AND THE TRACES OF AUTOBIOGRAPHY

If Barthes, in his rejection of autobiographical convention, wrote a fragmented autobiography, Jacques Derrida goes one step further and scatters autobiography as a motif or theme throughout his work. As we have already seen, Derrida's commentary on Rousseau's *Confessions* in *On Grammatology* points to the impossibility of Rousseau ever fulfilling his avowed aim of self-presence in this text, diverted as he is into the inevitable mediations and displacements of writing. Autobiography as a demand for unmediated selfhood is, it seems, doomed to reiterate itself endlessly as text. In a later essay, 'To Speculate – on "Freud"', and starting from a different direction, from a text which is not explicitly autobiographical, Derrida nevertheless finds autobiography at work deconstructing its supposed rational or theoretical basis. Taking Freud's *fort–da*, the famous scene in *Beyond the Pleasure Principle* where Freud describes his grandson Ernst playing with a reel, throwing it away and recovering it while at the same time uttering the words *fort* (there) and *da* (here), Derrida sees autobiography as the unwitting replication by the text of the process it is trying, rationally, to understand. Freud is also performing a *fort–da* by recalling the scene of his grandson's play, who is himself, with the aid of the reel, recalling his mother. According to Derrida, Freud is doing with his text what Ernst is doing with his reel: he is recalling himself, just as Ernst is, but through a substitutive process – a supplementary operation – which can never be complete and which he can never completely master. Moreover, the scene opens up a series of genealogical permutations – grandson and grandfather, daughter and mother – whereby the substitution of places happens within an already existing chain of family relations: Ernst's mother becomes Freud's mother but she is already his daughter. Derrida characteristically employs puns in order to enact this plurality and at the same time illustrate Freud's always incomplete mastery of the text. For Derrida the point is that the *fort–da* is never simply the theory Freud supposes, but a process inscribed by the text in advance. The string the child plays with is also the descendant, son or grandson (*fils*); the net (*filet*) is already in place, and by pulling on the string (*fils*) Freud inevitably gets caught up: 'He himself has been caught in advance by the catching' (Derrida 1991: 548).

Derrida's frequent returns to the problem of autobiography in his writing signal its importance to him as an 'irritant' (Smith 1995: 5), troubling the border between the 'life' and the 'work'. While the autobiographical subject (as in Rousseau's *Confessions*, for instance) is always engaged in going beyond itself into other discourses, or into discourse as a form of otherness, philosophical discourse is seen by Derrida as dependent on moments which defy its own systematic coherence, a specificity, or autobiographical trace, which remains despite the assumption of universality, and which it can never decisively overcome. Instead of using 'autobiography' in a familiar sense, as a genre with a history and already recognizable conventions and form, Derrida wants to think about autobiography as operating in a new space in a completely different way. For Derrida the point is that once one problematizes the border, once the life and the work become difficult to separate and the status of empirical facts as they apply to an author's life or his 'corpus', his works, is thrown into question, then the autobiographical also has to be 'redistributed' or 'restructured'. Autobiography still exists, Derrida is careful to point out, but its meaning will not be the same (Derrida 1988: 45).

Derrida's reformulation of the problem of the autobiographical has many ramifications; however, two in particular seem important here. The first is his rethinking of the role of the signature, the 'proper name' or autograph, and the way it inhabits that problematic borderline between life and work; the second, not unrelated, is his redefining of autobiography as 'thanatography' (*thanatos* Gk. – death), a writing not of a living but a dead author. For Derrida the question of the proper name or signature quickly takes on overtones of death since the name with which one signs will always outlive the bearer of that name. Indeed, to the extent that the proper name has a life of its own, it proclaims the death of its bearer every time it is used:

> In calling or naming someone while he is alive, we know that his name can survive him and already survives him; the name begins during his life to get along without him speaking and bearing his death each time it is inscribed in a list, or a civil registry, or a signature.
>
> (Derrida 1988: 49)

Therefore, since autobiography doubles the attempt to live through the name by also taking the name into the title of the work, it also increases its own involvement with death. In attempting to make use of the name as a guarantee of self-presence, autobiography is deflected further from its aim, overrun by the death it releases through writing.

Derrida has exemplified many of these ideas in his exploration of Nietzsche's autobiographical text, *Ecce Homo* (1899). Taking Nietzsche's exergue, a single page which is situated between the Preface and the first chapter, and which is dated as written on his forty-fifth birthday, the day on which, as Nietzsche sees it, he 'buries' his forty-fourth year, knowing that the achievements of that year, his writings, are 'immortal', Derrida finds Nietzsche's own idea of the 'eternal return' inscribed in the 'strange present' of this autobiographical moment (Derrida 1988: 13). Nietzsche affirms his own life by imagining it as a gift for which he feels grateful: '"How could I fail to be grateful to my whole life? – and so I tell my life to myself."' This statement of autobiographical intent is not autobiographical in the way commonly understood by the term, according to Derrida; it is not autobiographical because the signatory recalls his past life from a point outside or beyond the text but because he is 'the addressee and destination' of the narration *within* the text. The 'I', therefore, only constitutes itself through a return; he does not sign prior to what he will have become through the texts he has written. The 'I' thus has no prehistory, no point of origin outside writing; rather 'I' is cited (recited) within the text: 'It is the eternal return that signs and seals' (ibid.).

For Derrida the exergue, and its exemplary placing *between* – between the title and the Preface on the one hand and the work to come on the other – says something about the problematic borderline of autobiography, neither inside the author's work nor his life; but never simply exterior to them either. This act of self-engendering – 'I tell my life to myself' – which is not one moment or place but structured through a return, an endlessly repeating gesture of affirmation, looping back on itself is an 'instantly vanishing limit', in Derrida's words, that disappears only to reappear again (Derrida 1988: 14). Moreover, within this structure of return, difference intervenes, for the 'I' who speaks does not coincide with 'myself' to whom my life is told. In order to hear myself speak my speech must pass through the labyrinthine passages of the ear; it must risk not being heard or being heard differently. In this sense the ear is always the ear of the other: the message I send cannot return unless I allow otherness to intervene, unless the circuit from mouth to ear is open for others to hear. It is this otherness which allows communication to occur. It is therefore the ear of the other, according to Derrida, that says 'me to me' (p.51); and it is according to this logic that the signature becomes effective not at the time it apparently takes place, but later, when the other, with ears to hear it, has understood my name or deciphered my signature: 'A text is signed only much later by the other' (ibid.).

The 'I' is always a place of self-division for Derrida, an addressor *and* an addressee, a name which, after it is spoken, also requires to be heard. Derrida finds another way of expressing this duality by turning to Nietzsche's 'riddle' of his family origins, his genealogy:

'I am, to express it in the form of a riddle, already dead as my father, while as my mother, I am still living and becoming old' (Derrida 1988: 15). This gendered division within the subject makes the father, or the name of the father, always the sign of death, while the mother lives on as the 'living feminine'. For Derrida, the mother and father signify the dual inheritances of language: the formal, scientific, dead paternal language and the 'natural, living mother tongue' (p.26). Language must pass through the body by way of the mouth and the ear; in this way it takes what is already dead and regenerates or revitalizes it as the 'living feminine'. The mother is a metaphor for what is not metaphoric about language. Hers is the body through which language must pass to make itself heard; hers is the impetus to difference and to specificity. However, the price of her positioning as the vital principle of language is that she herself does not live or speak. She is fundamental but she is also anonymous:

> She gives rise to all the figures by losing herself in the back-ground of the scene like an anonymous persona. Everything comes back to her, beginning with life; everything addresses and destines itself to her. She survives on the condition of remaining at bottom.
>
> (Derrida 1988: 38)

This statement provokes a number of questions about women's relation to writing, and to autobiography in particular, which I will pursue in the next section. For the moment, however, it is important to think a little more about Derrida's positioning of the mother. What happens, for instance, when Derrida writes autobiographically about his own mother, as he does in 'Circumfession' (1993)? How does his autobiographical address to the mother relate to his theoretical placing of her? And is it significant that 'Circumfession', the most explicitly autobiographical of Derrida's texts to date, should open, like Barthes' *Cameria Lucida*, on the painful scene of the mother's dying?

As we have already seen, 'Circumfession' is a text which is also about Saint Augustine's *Confessions*, and which therefore imbricates another's autobiography in its own. Derrida's text runs along the bottom of the pages of a 'masterful' outline of his work by the critic Geoffrey Bennington which dominates the readerly space. Autobiography, so this multiplicity of discourses suggests, already has a relation to other texts; there is no singular text of the self or no autobiography which is only one's own. However, this positioning of Derrida's text also suggests the way reason fails to comprehend or master the autobiographical or the contingent, which troubles its borders with some other, unassimilated meaning. Derrida writes and tries to preserve the unpredictable, which is necessarily absent from Bennington's text about him. He engages in a 'duel' with him which he can never finally win. Who owns the name Derrida? This is the same question that Derrida asked in respect of Nietzsche when he discovered that the other must always sign in his place. Now he suggests a struggle to preserve what cannot be preserved; his challenge is to return what is not possible, the living body or life to the text; to say something uncodifiable which will disrupt Bennington's text, a text which, by turning him into a system of thought, has also forgotten him. To forget, in this instance, means surrendering to the law, leaving out of account the living presence.

Derrida also writes 'Circumfession' to his mother; he tries to reclaim his name from Bennington in order to give it back to his mother, but a mother who no longer recognizes him:

> I am writing here at the moment when my mother no longer recognizes me, and at which, still capable of speaking or articulating, a little, she no longer calls me and for her and therefore for the rest of her life I no longer have a name. . . . I am writing for my mother, perhaps even for a dead woman and so many analogies or recent analogies will come to the reader's mind even if no, they don't hold, those analogies, none of them, for if

I were here writing for my mother, it would be for a living mother who does not recognize her son.

(Derrida 1993: 25)

Derrida's writing turns personal in its turn to the mother: he offers up his name to her who no longer recognizes him. In trying to reach towards his mother he must lose himself, since she, almost bereft of language, can no longer recall him. Derrida's interminable sentences in 'Circumfession' seem to be trying to prolong the moment before the end, to postpone the death that is also coming. In a sense the mother's death is unthinkable because it is she who underwrites his name with her body, who guarantees his name by providing him with his ground or being. Derrida invokes the ritual of circumcision and the blood shed from the body during what is also, within Jewish tradition, a ceremony of naming, in order to try to rejoin the text to the living body. The mother's role within circumcision has been to sacrifice the son to the social, to offer up his body for the sake of the name, but to weep for him and feel a pain which the social can never recognize. Derrida tries to imagine an impossible writing which, in a sense this autobiography is, which might include blood, with the pen as a kind of syringe, drawing out the invisible inside (Derrida 1993: 10); however, writing always presupposes that a separation from the body has already occurred, that it comes after circumcision, the sacrifice of the body, when the blood has already been shed. To think of circumcision is also to think of a moment when her prayers and tears are mingled with his blood; his pain now recalls her pain for him then, a pain or mourning which, however, she cannot express. In trying to speak to her or for her, it seems Derrida always speaks in her place. Indeed when the mother appears in Derrida's text it is in terms of a body which is shamefully exposed, decaying, or already dead. He, in a sense, cannot represent her without doing violence to her, which in turn – and there is a repetition here of the way *she* becomes *him* – recalls the violence inflicted on his own body. Derrida tries to rescue his mother from death through a writing, which, however close it tries to come to her and to the body, will speak only of death. This, for Derrida, is the dilemma of autobiography, which is always posited in terms of an impossibility: the mother he addresses, who draws forth this mournful, autobiographical text from him, also does not recognize him. Pain and the risk of fragmentation are evident in this text which pushes itself to the boundary of what can be said. But it also leaves us with questions. Can the mother exist only on condition – and as the condition – of the son's speech? Does autobiography depend on her living on but staying mute? Can she never speak for herself? This, the problem of women's relation to autobiography, now needs to be addressed in the next section.

FEMINISM AND POSTSTRUCTURALISM

Feminist critics writing about autobiography in the 1980s encountered an obvious gap: the absence of women's texts from an accepted canon of autobiographical writing, a canon which, as we have already seen, placed the 'confessional' texts of Saint Augustine and Rousseau at its centre. As with other genres, it was not that women did not produce autobiographical writing but that it was deemed to be unimportant, crude or illegitimate, to fail to live up to the necessary test of 'great writing'. In her Introduction to the collection of essays which inaugurated criticism of women's texts, *Women's Autobiography: Essays in Criticism*, Estelle Jelinek picked up on a male critic's hostile response to Kate Millet's autobiography *Flying* (1979) with the comment: '"Insignificant," indeed, expresses the predominant attitude of most critics towards women's lives' (Jelinek 1980: 4). The slippage from 'text' to 'life' is instructive and helps to define a weakness in this early approach. If male critics had too easily conflated the description of a genre with a narrative of the masculine subject, feminist critics sought validation for women's experience in a not dissimilar way, by using autobiographical texts as reference for life. The notion of a pre-existing self underlying the text and accessed by it bypasses the problem of who the subject is and how she is constituted. For Domna Stanton, what was at stake in women's autobiography was not the recuperation of identities nor what she dismissed as a 'facile assumption of referentiality' but the difference within women's writing: the female autograph dramatizes alterity and non-presence she believes 'even as it asserts itself discursively and strives towards an almost impossible self-possession' (Stanton 1984: 16).

'Difference' is the term that is used to replace the notion of gendered identity as something innate, drawing attention instead to how 'masculine' and 'feminine' are meanings produced within and through language. Since language is 'phallocentric', that is, it subsumes the feminine into a masculine 'universal', women's difference is produced in terms of an absence or gap within language, which can also be used as a subversive space. For Mary Jacobus the late 1970s was the time when poststructuralist theory with its critique of 'essentialized' identities 'infiltrated and often polarized' feminist criticism (Jacobus 1986: x). By the 1980s there was a growing acknowledgement that 'difference', just like 'identity' to which it was first opposed, could also become reified and abstract: after all, there might be both political and theoretical dangers for feminism in ignoring both the context and the strategic usefulness of 'identities'. Rather than simply seeing the debate between identity and difference repeated in relation to autobiography with earlier criticism being discredited or, at least, recomplicated, by later poststructuralist theory, it is also important for us to recognize here the part played by autobiography in changing or reconfiguring the theoretical issues. Autobiography has been one of the most important sites of feminist debate precisely because it demonstrates that there are many different ways of writing the subject. The turn to autobiographical texts within feminism, therefore, also enabled critics to replay the problem of the subject in ways that are often experimental, which seemed to lie outside the terms of theory as it was currently thought.

Nancy Miller, who came from a backgound in French theory, gave a new turn to the argument in 1985 when she voiced the view that the radical potential of poststructuralism had dissipated itself in its own tendency to universalize and to fetishize difference. The 'dead' author, instead of vacating the role formally occupied by the unitary subject of humanist ideology, was still a powerfully gendered presence, according to Miller, inhibiting the recognition of its others. Miller's dissent was based on the belief that the concept of the author was always inflected by a history and, what is more, a history which had been notably different for women than for men:

> The postmodernist decision that the Author is Dead and the subject along with him does not, I will argue, necessarily hold for women, and prematurely forecloses the question of agency for them. Because women have not had the same historical relation of identity to origin, institution, production that men have had, they have not, I think, (collectively) felt burdened by too much Self, Ego, Cogito, etc.
>
> (Miller 1988: 106)

Nicole Ward Jouve expressed a similar point when she suggested the prematurity for women of deconstructing a subject which had not yet been allowed to instate itself: 'You must have a self before you can afford to deconstruct it' (Jouve 1991: 7). For the moment these insights, applied to autobiography, raised the fear of women again being consigned to an 'unrecoverable absence' in a new, but, as it turns out, no less problematic, theoretical mode. Could women risk their removal as authors without betraying their own feminist political agenda? Should an autobiography not be able to offer the woman reader a form of validation for herself, 'the assurance and consolation that she does indeed exist in the world', as Bella Brodski and Celeste Schenk put it? This satisfaction was what readers were being deprived of by poststructuralist theory and 'a femininity defined in purely textual terms' (Brodski and Schenk 1988: 14).

Perhaps, most importantly for these critics, it was precisely the 'bios' part of autobiography, that referentiality which had been excluded from Stanton's definition of autobiography, which gave access to a range of *differences* in terms of material lives, which the generalizing term, difference, obscured. Liz Stanley agreed: for her, readers read autobiography for many, complex reasons, but one of the most important was to find out about other people's lives; one way of reading autobiography, therefore, was to read it as biography. This was connected for Stanley to the feminist argument that it was politically necessary to recognize the plurality of women's lives rather than privilege through theory one (inevitably Western and middle-class) notion of Woman. 'The differences of women's lives matter, not differences from an assumed exemplary male life, but rather differences from each other' (Stanley 1992: 120).

To be fair, Derrida, who is so often cited as the critical opponent, had also perceived the dangers in the 1970s of a feminist agenda based on a singular concept of Woman: 'There is no one woman, no one truth in itself about woman in itself' (Derrida 1991: 372–3). As we have seen, his notion of autobiography also extends beyond the question of the subject – its constructedness and alterity – to the life, understood not as an object or a narrative, something, therefore, that we have already distanced ourselves from, but as a 'living principle', troubling the status and boundaries of the written text. Both 'woman', and autobiography with which she is sometimes conflated, can act as 'levers of intervention', subverting the logic of identity and exposing how a text's margins and limits are also inscribed within it (Feder *et al.* 1997: 2). However, the question remains how far Derrida's deconstruction of woman's position in one masculinist philosophical system merely entraps her in another. As Ellen K. Feder and Emily Zakin point out in a recent collection of essays entitled *Derrida and Feminism*, Derrida begins his interrogation of Nietzsche in *Spurs* with the statement: 'it is woman who will be my subject', and, however much she is the 'locus' for the displacement of phallogocentrism, she is still, as the possessive pronoun indicates, 'the servant to Derrida's interrogation': 'Women have always been exchanged in the service of men's subjectivity. Derrida may simply be offering a new twist to an old theme: he exchanges women in the service of the deconstruction of men's subjectivity.' For these critics there is an important distinction, which Derrida can be seen to elide, between 'the question of woman' and 'women's questions', between woman as his subject and her own (Feder *et al.* 1997: 41).

This argument does not necessarily mean falling back into essentialism, the presumption that we already know what 'woman' 'is'. As Barbara Johnson argues: 'Just because identities are fictions does not mean that they have not had, and could not have, real historical effects' (Johnson 1994: 72). Or, just because essentialism is philosophically discredited or deconstructed does not mean that it has lost its power to form past and present understandings of sexual difference or that it is not still, as Diane Elam argues, 'very much part of institutional practices' . The question is, therefore, not what it means to be a woman, but the 'pragmatic force' of institutional readings of 'sexual markings' (Elam 1994: 64). The body has a *political* meaning which is stubbornly resistant to its destabilization; or, as Barbara Johnson puts it: 'Being positioned as a woman is not something that is entirely voluntary' (Johnson 1987: 3).

There remains, therefore, if our emphasis shifts to the future, a *political* imperative for women to consitute themselves as subjects if they are to escape being never-endingly determined as objects. This need not mean returning to the same (masculine) subjectivity which saw itself as unitary and complete, simply expanding it to include women within its definition, but rather imagining multiple subjectivities, which are without foundation but located, instead, in particular times and places. Within this project, autobiography has an important role. For Diane Elam, 'the genre of women's auto-biography should be understood as a strategic necessity at a particular time, rather than an end in itself' (Elam 1994: 65). As *strategy*, autobiography need not offer a universal model of subjectivity and its representation but 'local uses of the self', ways of expressing a self or a position which 'arises from the situation as it comments on it' (Probyn 1993: 98). Writing about Latin American women's testimonies, Elspeth Probyn sees the self in this writing as making something appear, 'a conjunctural document of the self and of the times' (Probyn 1993: 98). The question is recast, therefore, in relation to autobiography, becoming not 'what is it' but instead 'what does it *do*'. For Regenia Gagnier there is a 'pragmatics of representation' where truth is less the issue than 'the purpose an autobiographical statement serves in the life and circumstances of its author and readers' (Gagnier 1991: 4). As we will see in the course of the next two chapters there are other subjects, beyond some ideal notion of 'the Subject', and other ways of reading autobiography.

3

OTHER SUBJECTS

GENDER, MODERNISM AND AUTOBIOGRAPHY

Virginia Woolf (1882–1941) was critically engaged all her life in the problem of writing lives and, in particular, the problem of writing women's lives. An important modernist writer of fiction, she also questioned from a feminist perspective traditional accounts of the subject and prefigured and even helped to influence present-day debates about writing and sexual difference. She provides a good place to begin a chapter about 'Other Subjects' and an important point of reference for all the debates about difference that follow.

Virginia Woolf's family connections – she was daughter of the editor of that nineteenth-century monument to egregious lives, *The Dictionary of National Biography*, Sir Leslie Stephen, and the inheritor of a family tradition of autobiographical writing, stretching back several generations – ensured her fascination with life-writing as well as sharpening her resistance to many of its assumptions and values. Her great-grandfather, James Stephen, had written his memoirs in the 1820s 'for the use of his children'; Sir Leslie Stephen, devastated by the death of his second wife Julia, Virginia Woolf's mother, similarly addressed his memoir of her, the *Mausoleum Book*, to their children conceiving of it as 'a little treasure to read for themselves when I have become a memory too' (Alan Bell 1977: x). As Trev Broughton points out, though thus restricting its audience to 'family' and defining itself as 'private', the *Mausoleum Book* also dictates 'the conditions and meaning of privacy itself' (Broughton 1999: 5); it thus recalls the way the father dominated the household, defining the space and the boundaries, after Julia's death. As Woolf was later to write, it was part of their 'duty' as children to encourage their father to talk and vent his grief, while they inhabited a 'stifling' silence: 'One had always to think whether what one was about to say was the right thing to say' (Woolf 1978a: 109). The *Mausoleum Book* sets out to commemorate Julia for her children but 'incidentally' turns the reader's attention to Stephen himself: 'I wish to write mainly about your mother. But I find that in order to speak intelligibly it will be best to begin by saying something about myself' (Alan Bell 1977: 4). The masculine narrative takes precedence over the feminine one; indeed by depicting her role as domestic angel and celebrating her unobtrusive 'feminine' virtues of care, he also endorses his own centrality; he becomes simultaneously the object of her concern and his readers'. The piety of 'remembering' Julia is thus waylaid by another, more dubious motive: to claim his children's sympathy for himself and reassert his central role as 'paterfamilias' for all the children, including, most crucially in terms of his future welfare, his stepdaughter, Stella (Broughton 1999: 67).

If Stephen's avowed aim to write about his wife as 'the main story' is pre-empted by his own needs and masculine viewpoint, the hesitations and obliquities of the *Mausoleum Book* reveal that nineteenth-century assumptions of gender – and genre – were not entirely straightforward: the need to relate to, if not quite relate, the other's story leaves traces which are never entirely expelled (Broughton 1999: 21). This is important when we come to consider

Woolf's own writing. One of her earliest attempts at autobiography, 'Reminiscences' (1908), emulates the family tradition by addressing itself to her sister Vanessa's first child Julian, and borrowing both scenes and language from her father's text. Woolf, however, quickly realizes that by memorializing her mother her writing turns lapidary, making her into a statue by fixing her or enshrouding her in words:

> Written words of a person who is dead or still alive tend most unfortunately to drape themselves in smooth folds annulling all evidence of life. You will not find in what I say, or again in those sincere but conventional phrases in the life of your grand-father, or in the noble lamentations with which he fills the pages of his autobiography, any semblance of a woman whom you can love.
>
> (Woolf 1978a: 41–2)

Woolf experimented all her life, in both her autobiography and fiction, with this problem of how to allow the mother's presence into a writing which has traditionally not permitted her a place. This carries echoes of Derrida's pursuit of the 'living feminine' within a language which excludes both the body and the mother. To suggest an affinity between Woolf's experimentation with language and literary form, and poststructuralist thinking, has become a commonplace in the last fifteen years: Woolf has emerged as a pre-eminent 'deconstructionist' feminist who, according to Toril Moi, 'reveals a deeply sceptical attitude to the male-humanist concept of an essential human identity' (Moi 1985: 9). As auto-biographer, Woolf produced unstable or provisional writing, sketches rather than formal memoirs, letters and a diary. These forms, and in particular her diary, became a way of constructing a different subject, a 'subject-in-process', to use Julia Kristeva's term, a subject which is not fixed but 'constantly called into question' (Kristeva 1989: 129). Her diary was conceived of by her as speculative, a writing towards a writing which has not yet happened:

There looms ahead of me the shadow of some kind of form
which a diary might attain to. I might in the course of time learn
what it is that one might make of this loose, drifting material
of life; finding another use for it than the use I put it to, so
much more consciously & scrupulously, in fiction. What sort of
diary should I like mine to be? Something loose knit, & yet not
slovenly, so elastic that it will embrace any thing, solemn, slight
or beautiful that comes into my mind.

(Woolf 1983: I, 266)

By imagining her diary as an unbounded space, no longer under the
control of the subject, she also creates a space for something new to
emerge; she defers meaning, opening up a space of difference within
discourse (Anderson 1997: 49). Woolf's imaginings and reimagin-
ings of space – the rooms and chambers of an uncharted unconscious
– always relate to the *possibility* of thinking femininity beyond the
certainty and closure demanded by what Woolf herself referred to
as 'the damned egotistical self' (Woolf 1983: II,14). It is only by
thinking outside the dominance of the letter 'I' which she wittily
figured in *A Room of One's Own* (1929) as a 'straight dark bar', lying
across the page and obscuring sight of anything and anyone else, that
one can begin to glimpse a different subject; one can begin to open
the question of the woman at the edges of the masculine text (Woolf
1977: 95).

To backtrack for a moment: Woolf took her bearings from her
father's work as biographer, but found herself intrigued by what she
called 'the lives of the obscure', the forgotten lives, mostly of women,
who had been marginalized by the *Dictionary*'s selection of 'great
men'. It was not always the case that these lives had gone unrecorded:
they could be glimpsed, like the woman above, in existing documents, and Woolf imagined herself turning the pages of dusty
and hidden volumes, rediscovering lives which have been relegated
to the backwaters – or shadows – of history (Woolf 1967: 120). Nor
was it a matter of making an alternative claim for their 'greatness';

rather Woolf used their 'obscurity' to interrogate the very terms in which the biographical subject is thought, challenging notions of the 'exceptional' or 'unique' as self-evidently connoting value and questioning whether progress and achievement provided the only ways of structuring historical understanding.

> It is one of the attractions of the unknown, their multitude, their vastness; for, instead of keeping their identity separate, as remarkable people do, they seem to merge into one another, their very boards and title-pages and frontispieces dissolving, and their innumerable pages melting into continuous years so that we can lie back and look up into the fine mist-like substance of countless lives, and pass unhindered from century to century, from life to life.
>
> (Woolf 1967: 122)

It is not possible to separate lives from books, or identities from how they are represented, Woolf suggests, and much of what we think of as 'true' or historically given, is really an ideological construct; in other words, a fiction.

As a novelist, Woolf self-consciously defined herself as 'modern', notoriously attacking her Edwardian predecessors, in particular Arnold Bennett, John Galsworthy and H.G.Wells, for their 'materialism', for missing the 'unlimited capacity and infinite variety' of the living person by concentrating on social detail: 'When all the practical business of life has been discharged, there is something about people which continues to seem to them of over-whelming importance' (Woolf 1983: 3, 388). She brought similar modernist preoccupations with the subjective to bear on biography, questioning whether the truth of a person could ever be equated with the external facts of their life. For Woolf Victorian biography was both artless and dull: it produced 'fossils' rather than 'living' people (Woolf 1967: 231). She tried to imagine a different kind of biography which could bring together fiction's attention to the 'intangible personality' and the 'inner life' with the veracity and substance of historical fact, which could somehow create, as she said, 'that queer amalgamation of dream and reality, that perpetual marriage of granite and rainbow' (p.235). As so often in Woolf's imagining of difference, the tense points to the future, to an unrealized potential which cannot be defined or contained within traditional structures. However, this does not mean that Woolf did not herself try to write biographies which mixed fact with fiction in exactly the way she describes. In a very early work, for instance, her unpublished 'Journal of Mistress Joan Martyn' (1906), she gives us a fictionalized account of a fifteenth-century woman's life, otherwise unrecorded in history. As in her brief biographical sketch of Shakespeare's sister in *A Room of One's Own* more than a decade later, she turns to fiction as the only way to remedy a historical absence. This also involves her in questioning the limits and authority of historical knowledge: by writing a fictional history she demonstrates how like fiction history is and how arbitrary and partial the distinction between them. Joan Martyn's journal also serves to insert into the historical account of lives an intensely subjective voice: biography must become autobiography in order to understand the 'inner life'. For the woman, living without external recognition, submerged in her husband's story, this becomes crucial: Joan Martyn tells of secret, inchoate desires:

> Yet what it is I want, I cannot tell, although I crave for it, and in some secret way, expect it. For often and oftener as time goes by, I find myself suddenly halting in my walk, as though I were stopped by a strange new look upon the surface of the land which I know so well. It hints at something; but it is gone before you know what it means; it half frightens you, and yet it beckons.
>
> (Woolf 1979: 256)

Hers is a story of becoming, of yearning and potential. For Woolf it makes the case for another hidden story residing within history, for the 'unlimited capacity and infinite variety' of the person which is always in excess of what is outwardly visible or recoverable through an account of external actions alone.

Woolf also wrote parodic versions of biography, drawing on the mock-heroic tones of Laurence Sterne's famously comic fictional life, *Tristram Shandy*, to deflate the pretensions of the form, as well as undermine the formal conventions which are used to sustain its 'truthfulness' (Briggs 1995: 251). *Orlando* is her most sustained effort at debunking: it is an irreverent, triumphantly fictive biography in which Woolf refuses to separate life and writing; Orlando's progress through the ages is also a history of writing, with Orlando's change of sex occurring at around the moment, during the reign of Charles I, when, according to Woolf, the woman writer historically comes into view. Towards the end of the novel, having arrived in the twentieth century, Orlando offers an autobiographical 'peroration' on the multiplicity of 'selves' which constitute her; the biographer as a result finds her own role 'discomposed':

> We must here snatch time to remark how discomposing it is for her biographer that this culmination and peroration should be dashed from us on a laugh casually like this; but the truth is that when we write of a woman, everything is out of place – culmi-nations and perorations; the accent never falls where it does with a man.
>
> (Woolf 1978b: 195)

Woman's difference, so Woolf suggests, requires a different emphasis; it flies in the face of conventional modes of representation, producing a multiplicity which cannot be captured within one and the same, the singular 'I' of masculine discourse. It also deprives the biographer of authority, displacing the notion of truth from one fiction to another: 'When we write of a woman, everything is out of place.' The biographer cannot simply contain the difference which the auto-biographical peroration makes to the narrative they are attempting

to tell; a 'natural' hierarchy of genders and genres has given way to
a more casual and unstable ordering.

Yet despite her own irreverence towards the conventions of
biography and her insistence on the entanglement of identities with
writing, Woolf, at the end of her life, did return to writing a more
factual autobiography, her remarkable 'Sketch of the Past' (1940),
which also remained significantly unfinished and unpublished. Her
sense of the problems inherent in what she is doing are never far from
the surface, however, and her 'Sketch' is precisely that, an experiment
or notes towards a composition that she might undertake in the
future. Like her diary, the 'Sketch' presents itself as 'improvisation',
a relief from the 'horrid labour' required to make 'an orderly and
expressed work of art' (Woolf 1978a: 87). Here Woolf was referring
in particular to her current work in writing a biography of Roger
Fry, a task she had undertaken at his family's request and to which
she found herself both temperamentally and theoretically unsuited.
The 'Sketch' then allows her to 'let fly' from a repressive present into
a different past; it opens up space or time for herself away from the
conventional ordering of biography 'where one thing follows another
and all are swept into a whole' (p.87).

In the 'Sketch' Woolf also returns to the problem of representing her mother which, as we have seen, she had first struggled
with more than thirty years before. Instead of writing in an 'objective' or 'distant' way about her mother as she had in her earlier
'Reminiscence', she now discovers new techniques of proximity,
ways of collapsing the distance which writing imposes between
herself and her mother's body, in order to recall her own beginnings.
Woolf opens the 'Sketch' with her first memory which is of
anemones, seen close up, on her mother's dress. This then leads to
another memory, which also seems, paradoxically, to be the first:

> It is of lying half asleep, half awake, in bed in the nursery at St.
> Ives. It is of hearing the waves breaking, one, two, one, two, and
> sending a splash of water over the beach; and then breaking,

one, two, one, two, behind a yellow blind. It is of hearing the
blind draw its little acorn across the floor as the wind blew the
blind out. It is of lying and hearing this splash and seeing this
light, and feeling, it is almost impossible that I should be here;
of feeling the purest ecstasy I can conceive.

(Woolf 1978a: 74–5)

This second moment with its powerfully evoked 'oceanic' feelings,
or feelings of boundlessness, symbolically echoes the first; the rhythm
of the waves, the repetition of breaks within a continuous flow,
also recalls the perception of the mother's dress with its bright,
particularized foreground against the dark background which holds
and contains it. Woolf is aware that these memories are primarily
'colour-and-sound memories' (Woolf 1978a: 77), archaic memories
which pre-date the 'naming' of the flowers as anemones as well as
the necessity, which language imposes, of giving her memories
a temporal order. Woolf is gesturing towards the pre-symbolic or
pre-Oedipal, the time, according to Lacan, before the subject is
constituted as such, before s/he takes up a position in language.
Trying to recall her mother, Woolf finds that she is both 'dispersed'
and 'omnipresent' (p.98), that 'one never got far enough away from
her to see her as a person' but that nevertheless she was 'central': 'She
was the whole thing. . . . She was keeping what I call in my short-
hand the panoply of life – that which we all lived in common – in
being' (p.96).

For Woolf her mother is most poignantly invoked in terms of the
'wholeness' which pre-existed her separation from her: her mother
contained her in just the way Woolf is attempting now to contain
her mother in writing. Like the 'obscure' who merge into each
other, breaking down what 'binds' them as separate, Woolf explores
a region of her 'self' which is indissociable from her mother before
the subject is stabilized within language. Woolf is therefore using
language to break down the certainties of language, to register the
jubilation but also later the terror that exists when the subject strays

towards the borders of subjecthood, when identity is called into question. Woolf describes here, in retrospect, when language is again able to reflect her, one such frightening moment of estrangement:

> That night in the bath the dumb horror came over me . . . that collapse I have described before; as if I were passive under some sledge-hammer blow; exposed to a whole avalanche of meaning that had heaped itself up and discharged itself upon me, unprotected, with nothing to ward it off . . . I could not explain it.
>
> (Woolf 1978a: 90–1)

Another such moment of self-fracturing happens when she sees her mother dead (Woolf 1978a: 106–7). Again Woolf introduces the memory as one of profound uncertainty. Did she see a man sitting beside her mother or was she merely pretending, in order to get attention? The memory is also about the instability of memory in the face of shock; without her mother there to reflect her she is not sure of what or who she sees; she doubts her self because her self is put in doubt. Significantly, the mother's death cannot be thought by the child without her hallucinating a presence which figures the strange otherness of her absence. There are things that cannot be remembered because the subject is not 'there' to remember them. In the 'Sketch', Woolf writes a memoir which is profoundly sceptical of what 'remembering' means. Instead of a subject who recalls the past from some stable place outside it, Woolf traces moments which slip from and exceed the conscious control of the subject, deciding that 'the things one does not remember are as important' as the things one does (Woolf 1978a: 80). Writing the self involves moments when the self is lost, when cracks appear and unconscious memory floods in: 'We are sealed vessels afloat on what it is convenient to call reality; and at some moments, the sealing matter cracks; in floods reality' (p.142). The self is never secure, nor can it form its own narrative. At best there are scenes or moments to return to which 'arrange themselves', and which are 'representative' or 'enduring' (ibid.). For Woolf the self is a construct which is known as much through its fragmentation as its unity. More than most writers she makes us aware of the process of flux and splitting which underlies, and constantly threatens, any notion of attained subjecthood.

LOCATING DIFFERENCE

Virginia Woolf has been a key figure for critics of autobiography who, drawing on the psychoanalytic writings of both Jacques Lacan and Julia Kristeva, have seen her writing as opening up the question of the feminine as a challenge to the phallic or masculine position of the subject. By conceiving of the subject as subject to dissolution and by exploring those fragmented, inchoate and repressed psychic realms, also coded within the symbolic as feminine, Woolf is seen as undermining the unity and confidence of that universal 'I' claimed by the masculine subject. For Shari Benstock, for instance, Woolf's 'Sketch' offers the primary example of how 'the self that would reside at the center of the text is decentered – and often absent altogether – in women's autobiographical texts' (Benstock 1988: 20). For Sidonie Smith, the 'Sketch' is a similarly radical and important text in which Woolf pursues 'a diffusive rather than unitary subjectivity' trying to 'dislodge the old "I" from autobiography': 'Everywhere the narrator of "Sketch" concedes the impossibility and the undesirability of the old autobiographical project . . . Woolf disperses herself into the past' (Smith 1993: 87, 100).

However, the emphasis by these critics on difference as simply *sexual difference*, as well as the codification of the feminine in terms of loss, absence and anonymity, has also been seen as problematic. Trev Broughton, for instance, suggests that 'the idea that women's self-constructions might be distinguished solely, or even mainly, on the basis of sexual difference – as the "other" of some putative universal "man"' – may be both 'reifying and essentialist' (Broughton and Anderson 1997: 97). The point being made is that the concept of sexual difference can itself become both monolithic and abstract, operating in effect as an alternative 'identity', rather than dislodging any such positivist notions. Julia Watson and Sidonie Smith have also recently argued that the privileging of gender oppression over other oppressions 'effectively erases the complex and often contradictory positionings of the subject' and can be seen as 'a central instance of the universalizing agenda of Western theorizing'. Instead they offer a view of the subject as multiply determined, occupying different locations in terms of gender, race, ethnicity and sexuality which 'one cannot easily sever, separate out, or subsume under one another' (Smith and Watson 1992: xiv). In this view the subject is constituted by gender but also by other divisions and representations which belong to specific histories and locations.

The argument that sexual difference, however useful it had been as an analytic tool in the 1970s and early 1980s, elided other forms of difference, belongs to a period, as Pheng Cheah and Elizabeth Grosz have argued, which saw the proliferation of 'new social movements', each with a specific focus or theme such as sexuality, race, ethnicity or class. The pluralization of difference within academic discourse, they suggest, thus 'also reflects and expresses . . . broader sociological and political events' (Cheah and Grosz 1998: 3). So far as autobiography is concerned, the deconstruction of it as a genre which privileged a white, masculine subject gave way, as part of this same moment of diversification, to a sense of its potential or use as political strategy by these new social groups. Julia Watson and Sidonie Smith have argued that the marginalized subject, by 'deploying autobiographical practices that go against the grain' can constitute 'an "I" that becomes a place of creative and, by implication, political intervention' (Smith and Watson 1992: xix). Julia Swindells has provided a more wide-ranging but similarly optimistic account of the new radical uses of autobiography:

> Autobiography now has the potential to be the text of the
> oppressed and the culturally displaced, forging a right to speak

> both for and beyond the individual. People in a position of
> powerlessness – women, black people, working-class people –
> have more than begun to insert themselves into the culture via
> autobiography, via the assertion of a 'personal' voice, which
> speaks beyond itself.
>
> (Swindells 1995: 7)

The idea that autobiography can become 'the text of the oppressed', articulating through one person's experience, experiences which may be representative of a particular marginalized group, is an important one: autobiography becomes both a way of testifying to oppression and empowering the subject through their cultural inscription and recognition.

Yet this politicization of the subject, though it addresses it, by no means solves the problem of 'difference', since the claim to speak for others is always problematic and can also elide further differences under an assumed representativity. An identification in terms of sexuality, for instance, may occlude other differences in terms of class or race. Nor can the marginalized subject simply escape the mediations of discourse, that inevitable troping or figuring of self-consciousness within autobiography which de Man described and saw as confusing its boundary with fiction. As Julia Swindells has argued elsewhere, the autobiographical self is not invented *ex nihilo* but constructed by 'calling on' the representations that are historically available and which may include fictional ones. Thus nineteenth-century working-class women, according to Swindells, turned to the novel, the melodrama or romance as models when they came to represent their own lives, as places where women were at least visible, albeit in a 'reified' or 'idealised' form (Swindells 1985: 11). That politicizing or 'rematerializing' of difference (Smith 1989: 315) which autobiography has been seen as undertaking is therefore always a complex matter involving both the subject's discursive position *and* material/historical location. While position and location are enfolded in each other they are not reducible to the same.

As cultural critic Stuart Hall has argued, discursive practices 'always implicate' the positions from which we speak and therefore 'though we speak, so to say "in our own name", of ourselves and from our own experience, nevertheless who speaks, and the subject who is spoken of, are never identical, never exactly in the same place' (Hall 1990: 222).

Zora Neale Hurston's autobiography, *Dust Tracks on the Road* (1942), which her biographer and editor Robert E. Hemenway has called 'one of the most peculiar autobiographies in Afro-American literary history' (Hemenway, in Hurston 1984: ix), provides us with an important text in which many of the problems of 'identity' and 'difference' outlined above can be seen as coming into play. Written reluctantly, at the behest of her publisher, its 'authenticity' and 'honesty' have frequently been called into question. Hurston notoriously omits much of her life from the text: she refuses to elaborate on her literary career and fails to mention her second marriage; though she traces her life back to its origins and even recounts the scene of her birth, she never provides a date. All this, according to Hemenway, is part of 'her general reluctance to locate personal experience in the common chronological record' which then feeds into a far more problematic historical and political evasiveness (p.x). Throughout her autobiography Hurston is more concerned with 'individuality' than she is with racial or gender identities and, while not oblivious to racial oppression, she refuses to speak as representative of her race, out of a common history of victimhood. In a chapter entitled 'My People! My People' she challenges this statement of belonging with her own belief in individual character: 'Light came to me when I realized that I did not have to consider any racial group as a whole. God made them duck by duck and that was the only way I could see them. I learned that skins were no measure of what was inside people' (Hurston 1984: 235). The enlightened view is to see beyond skin colour to individual differences, and this extends to both white and black: 'Therefore I saw no curse in being black, nor no extra flavor by being white' (ibid.).

For those critics and writers who, from the 1970s onwards, have claimed that Afro-American autobiography is a specific sub-genre, providing an alternative place of self-identification based on collectivity, Hurston's seems a disappointing text. Stephen Butterfield, one of the first critics to write about 'black autobiography', believes that autobiography is 'one of the ways that black Americans have asserted their right to live and grow' and that these autobiographies conceive of the subject as 'a member of an oppressed social group, with ties and responsibilities to the other members' (Butterfield 1974: 2–3). The emergence of a black feminist criticism in the 1970s which explored representations of black women's lives has also posited the centrality of 'group identity', 'inter-dependence' and a respect for 'voice-enabling traditions' (McKay, in Brodski and Schenk 1988: 179). bell hooks, for instance, has argued for the political importance of 'honest confessional narratives by black women who are struggling to be self-actualized and to become radical subjects' in order to provide 'texts which affirm our fellowship with each other' (hooks 1992: 59). What we see again is autobiography being turned to as a way of providing 'truthful' depictions of life, albeit now from a radical perspective.

While Hurston has often been celebrated as a literary 'foremother' by contemporary Afro-American women writers and, in particular, by Alice Walker, who wrote of *Their Eyes Were Watching God* that 'there is no book more important to me than this one', her autobiography has seemed anomalous, even embarrassing: 'For me, the most unfortunate thing Zora ever wrote is her autobiography. After the first several chapters, it rings false' (Walker 1984: 91, 86). *Dust Tracks on the Road*, indeed, can only be accommodated within black autobiography's emancipatory project, that teleological narrative of 'becoming a self', in negative terms, as compromising in its attempt to placate its white readers, or as belonging to a historical moment when self-acceptance proved impossible for Afro-American women. However, it could equally be argued that the use of autobiography to create and affirm an identity for a particular group also relies on encoding a particular readership and on employing a discourse linking community and selfhood which is also, ultimately, a historical discourse. In other words, autobiography might be said always to involve strategies of representation, even if, for political reasons, at this particular historical juncture, it has re-appropriated the language of confession or truth.

Dust Tracks on the Road is a difficult text to situate within the 'radical' tradition of black autobiography because, as several critics have shown, instead of claiming an identity Hurston deliberately draws attention to the autobiographical self as a fiction. Early on, in an image which recalls Virginia Woolf's uneasiness about turning her mother into a statue, Hurston describes how self-representation is always at odds with our mundane selves; indeed that it monumentalizes a self which is absent, or never existed: 'People are prone to build a statue of the kind of person that it pleases them to be. And few people want to be forced to ask themselves, "What if there is no me like my statue?"' (Hurston 1984: 34). Hurston accordingly gives us various 'poses' for herself or allegorical moments which position her in relation to her reader. One of the most resonant of these is from childhood when she stations herself as 'watcher' on the 'seat on top of the gate-post', at the threshold of black and white worlds: 'Often the white travelers would hail me, but more often I hailed them, and asked, "Don't you want me to go a piece of the way with you?"' (p.45). This not only emblematizes her own position within the autobiography as observer and interpreter, mediating the black world for white readers; it also signals her refusal of the boundaries which assign her exclusively to one place or the other: Hurston reserves the right 'innocently' to sit somewhere between and to decide for herself which direction she will take.

According to Barbara Johnson, Hurston's work was 'constantly dramatizing and undercutting . . . inside / outside oppositions', a spatial complexity she also translated into the 'complex transactions of discursive exchange' (Johnson 1986: 318). Hurston also refuses to be placed linguistically: she moves across different 'languages', the universalizing language of standard English, an anthropological 'scientific' language, a highly metaphoric language and the folksy language of black oral tradition. In this passage, from the last chapter, 'Looking Things Over', Hurston celebrates the mixed nature of life, refusing to see herself as victim. Though she has been 'in Sorrow's kitchen and licked out all the pots', she nevertheless takes 'no refuge from myself in bitterness. To me, bitterness is the under-arm odor of wishful weakness. . . . I have no urge to make any concessions like that to the world as yet' (Hurston 1984: 280). Mixing aphorism and reflection, this passage also uses the body as a source of metaphor to enliven her language. If life is a mixture of different experiences, 'sharp shadows, high lights and smudgy inbetweens' (ibid.) which offers no stable, universal or transcendent perspective, but numerous instances of 'human self-bias' (Hurston 1984: 281), language is similarly fluid, shifting across a variety of registers, and mixing colourful individual and local usages with 'rational' but bland discourse (Smith 1993: 118). Hurston, as she says, is 'of the word-changing kind' (Hurston 1984: 27). Trained as an anthropologist and educated into middle-class language, Hurston discovers that, in order to elicit the material she wants she must learn to speak the language of her informants, to 'tell the tales, sing the songs, do the dances, and repeat the raucous sayings and doings of the Negro farthest down' (p.177). If she discovers that she must leave the constraining environment of her childhood in order to see both it and herself clearly, she also learns to value its specific culture and language: each language adds to her knowledge of the other as she moves fluidly between them, 'forever shifting' (p.117) without any settled 'home'. Refusing the boundaries of race and class and the notion of a settled identity, Hurston's freedom is also a form of linguistic expansiveness: 'Lord, give my poor stammering tongue at least one taste of the whole round world, if you please, Sir' (p.331). The voice of this appeal is the 'black' voice of her childhood; it now joins, however, with the universalizing language of political and philosophical reflection in a vivid enactment of her meaning.

Hurston's homelessness or 'wandering' is related back by her to the death of her mother which, for Hurston, as for Woolf, disrupted the world 'which had been built out of her body and her heart' (Hurston 1984: 89). The description of her mother's death again constructs an almost allegorical scene in which Hurston is crucially positioned in relation to her community. The inheritor of a burden of guilt, Hurston is given the responsibility of speaking for the silent mother, thus prefiguring her future role as writer. When she is too ill to talk, her mother, according to Hurston, 'looked at me, or so I felt, to speak for her. She depended on me for a voice' (pp.86–7). The mother had previously charged the 9-year-old Hurston with defying the folk customs of veiling the mirror and removing the pillow from her when she is dying: Hurston's guilt is that she is not strong enough to resist her community but, as child, is forced to give in. The mother, this scene suggests, requires the daughter's speech in order to oppose the community which will obscure her reflection and remove her imprint. Hurston is situated in a complex place, at the intersections of gender and history: she can only rescue the mother by transcending her mother's silent association with the body and defying the community which refuses her recognition. Neverthess it is the voices of her community which provide her with the language to describe and understand the experience of death. Language, significantly, has a double function, both connecting and separating her from her mother and the community. It is also what puts her into motion as a subject, allowing her to avoid the 'wordless feeling' she associates forever after with death (p.116).

Valerie Smith has argued that it is 'striking' how, when Anglo-American feminists have begun to reconsider 'the material ground of their enterprise', they have turned to the experiences and writings of black women in a move which disturbingly reproduces nineteenth-century cultural associations of black women with the body and thus 'with animal passions and slave labour' (Smith 1989: 316). As we have seen, *Dust Tracks on the Road*, with its flamboyant foregrounding of language and refusal of racialized identity, has tended to frustate such a critical move: Hurston is wary of any collapse back into the body or the community which might 'fix' her in one place and close off the 'horizon' she had directed her 'self' towards from childhood. However, if Hurston's autobiography maintains a gap or distance between language and experience, this does not mean that her writing simply transcends her historical and social situation to speak 'universally'. Barbara Johnson, for instance, has suggested that Hurston turned her life into a 'trickster tale', deriving her mode from the traditions of story-telling, 'lying' or improvisation, which she studied, where even the teller might not know the 'truth' (Johnson 1986: 328). This is important if we are not to see Hurston as simply 'decentring' the subject in general poststructuralist terms, in accordance with a totalizing theory which elides her specificity and difference. As Johnson argues, the terms 'black' and 'white', 'inside' and 'outside', still matter, even though their reference is difficult to determine (ibid.). It was Hurston's desire to evade the (white) reader's need to fix her in an identity by keeping on the move through discourses, through identities. History, therefore, was already at work *within* her strategies of displacement. Her 'unfixing of identity' could thus be said to challenge the ways we have of describing the subject's specificity and historical locatedness, without necessarily denying their ultimate importance.

LANDSCAPE FOR A GOOD WOMAN

In her book *Sexing the Self* (1993), Elspeth Probyn has put forward an important case for autobiography as a particular strategy or *use* of the self which can make productive links between discourse and material location. The question for Probyn is whether a particular autobiographical speaking position can be sustained without it solidifying into an identity, with all the problems of privilege and exclusion that that raises. She asks whether stories can 'be told through selves and through emotions without being at the expense of other stories and selves' (Probyn 1993: 84). In other words, in terms of the argument we have been pursuing, can the self eschew its representativeness, its role of 'speaking for others' and still have something of political significance to say? Can it move beyond the personal? For Probyn, the answer lies in recognizing the 'very mediated' nature of the speaking subject, the fact that self-representation is always developed in terms of the available conventions and discourses: for Probyn there is never 'a transparent self who speaks from the heart' (p.86). At the same time, however, it may also be possible to be aware of how the self can function as a 'lived moment' disrupting 'the smooth articulation of discursive systems': the self may thus also draw attention to discursive limits, to a lack of fit between itself and discourse, through which the historicity and locatedness of the discourses themselves come into view. The self which Probyn envisages is thus like an 'image' through which we are able to think where we are; it becomes 'a point of view into its own work as an articulation of the real and the discursive' (pp.88, 92).

Probyn turns to Carolyn Steedman's complex autobiographical text, *Landscape for a Good Woman* (1986) to illustrate her ideas. Steedman is primarily interested in how the specificities of class are eliminated from the dominant theoretical discourses, and uses her 'self' and her autobiography in much the way Probyn describes to question their limits. For Steedman, the powerful stories we tell about the family, drawing on sociology or psychoanalysis, often present their 'constituents' as neutral, though they actually use 'socially specific images' for their construction, the objects which derive from the bourgeois household and which become 'the system of everyday metaphors by which we see ourselves and our past' (Steedman 1986: 75, 77). Her own method is to use the images deriving from her experience to question the 'truths' of theory.

One of the most significant images or autobiographical memories that she describes is of her father picking bluebells and then being caught and humiliated by the forest-keeper. Such a memory, as

Steedman notes, does not fit well with the theory of patriarchy, the generalized account of the centrality of the father's role within the family and culture. Steedman depicts herself in adulthood wondering 'how the myth works when a father is rendered vulnerable by social relations, when a position in a household is not supported by recognition of social status and power outside it' (Steedman 1986: 72). For Steedman her memories are not so much individualized instances of some general truth as an 'interpretive device' (p.28), a way of interrogating the relation between individual experience and theoretical problems. The memory allows the past reality to be reflected upon and its specific social configuration to come into view. Another central image for Steedman is her mother in the 'New Look, a coat of beige gaberdine which fell in two swaying, graceful pleats from her waist at the back' (ibid.). This image is used by Steedman as a way of understanding her mother's desire and frustrations and their formation within specific class and economic terms. It also allows her to 'see' her relationship with her mother as the passing on of a 'deprivation' which is both material and psychological. The image is a dream image, but the dream image, now recalled, allows Steedman to understand a social landscape. Understanding herself then, as a child, seeing herself 'in the picture' also allows her to move the child into historical time. The social understanding of adulthood can then be focused back on the image allowing her to understand it further. Picturing the self allows entry into the social, without losing specificity and individuality; instead Steedman opens up a dialogue between the 'dream' and 'reality'.

For Steedman subjectivity is always implicated in the social, in the specificities of 'place and politics' (Steedman 1986: 6). This is powerfully dramatized in her representation of her mother's death and her particular naming of it as a 'working-class death':

Simone de Beauvoir wrote of her mother's death, said, that in spite of the pain it was an easy one: an upper-class death. Outside, for the poor, dying is a different matter. . . .

> Like this: she flung up her left arm over her head, pulled her knees up, looked out with an extraordinary surprise. She lived alone, she died alone: a working-class life, a working-class death.
>
> (Steedman 1986: 2)

It is worth noting briefly that, in all three of the autobiographies by women that we have looked at, the mother's death forms a central moment. As we have seen in the previous chapter, when looking at autobiographical texts by Barthes and Derrida, the mother's death may have a particular significance for the writing of autobiography. For Barthes and Derrida autobiography is on the side of the feminine, and their mournful accounts of the mother's dying is also a way of preserving her body within the body of their writing. In psychoanalytic accounts of the subject, on which both Barthes and Derrida draw, the 'I' is founded on separation and the loss of the mother's body: by identifying autobiographically with the mother – and identifying autobiography with the mother – they, as it were, bleed emotionally into their texts, opening up a wound in the self which is also a space for her. Is this also true for the women autobiographers we have looked at?

According to Julia Kristeva since 'I am she', it is much more difficult for the woman symbolically to 'kill' the mother and there is much more danger that she will identify with the 'dead one' who has been abandoned within herself (Kristeva 1989: 29–30). We might argue, therefore, that women become autobiographers *against* this identification with the mother and by triumphing over the threat of depression. What the texts we have looked at share in writing about the mother's death is a preoccupation with the imagery of seeing and reflection – with mirrors and screens – which could also suggest a disturbing specular identification with both the mother and her absence. Forced to contemplate the mother's absence, the 'I' risks seeing its own negation in the mirror. Do these texts thus provide insights into the writing of sexual difference?

Possibly; but Steedman challenges us also to see the differences *between* them in the local settings and emotions they describe. In Woolf's 'Sketch', therefore, looked at from this point of view, the nurse, the candles, the formal visit to the deathbed and the rituals of laying out and mourning all begin to take on a particular historical and social meaning. Hurston describes the superstitions which surround death and the very public nature of her mother's dying in a way which also evokes a particular cultural setting. Steedman helps to remind us that these details matter, are resonant of both time and place and help to form subjectivity; they establish a difference which is lost or ignored in the 'grand' narratives of sexual difference. Steedman also helps us to perceive that the mother is not just the primordial 'Other' who is incorporated into the subject but also a socially specific subject, who exists beyond the (psychoanalytic) narrative of her loss. The m(Other) is not just a metaphor, in other words; she is also a social subject whose difference and specificity needs to be recognized and found a place in our thinking.

POSTCOLONIAL SUBJECTS

It is central to both Elspeth Probyn's and Carolyn Steedman's argument that discursive positions and material locations are imbricated in each other, without ever forming a unity or a connection that is necessarily absolute and unchanging. However, we now need to ask what happens when the very notion of 'location' starts to change, when 'place' becomes layered with numerous crossings. For postcolonial critics the idea of 'hybridity' has become an extremely important one in trying to understand the kind of mobility, cross-over and diaspora generated by colonialism. Colonial rule, of course, was premised on notions of racial and cultural 'purity' and on preserving the 'difference' between the colonizers and colonized. As Ania Loomba observes, 'in practice, it did not necessarily work in that way' (Loomba 1998: 174), and colonialism instead provided the impetus for numerous cross-overs, genetic, intellectual and discursive. Homi Bhabha has described the way in which colonial discourse was itself split, producing a form of colonial mimicry, a set of resemblances which are never quite the same, and which implicitly question the homogeneity of the 'original' practices and discourses. Hybridity is produced as an effect of colonial power which must endlessly produce difference in order to justify its authority, and can never return to a 'wholeness' which exists prior to the colonial encounter. According to Bhabha, 'the colonial presence is always ambivalent, split between its appearance as original and authoritative and its articulation as repetition and difference' (Bhabha 1986: 169). Paul Gilroy has drawn attention to the significant displacement or movement of black peoples across the Atlantic which produced new diasporic cultures. This historical emphasis, as Gilroy explains, also requires a new way of theorizing identity, unhooking it from nationhood and ethnicity, and thinking instead of the more difficult theoretical option of 'creolisation, metissage, mestizaje, and hybridity' (Gilroy 1993: 2). As Ania Loomba suggests, there is 'no such thing as an uncontaminated white or European culture'; neither, however, is there an ethnically and culturally stable black identity, an essential identity that we can link to a point or place of origin (Loomba 1998: 176).

Postcolonial 'identity' could be seen as a contradiction in terms, therefore, seeming to arrest the movement of differences and gather under one heading a multiplicity of countries and locations. However, as we have seen, the lack of an essentialized identity does not rule out the possibility of constructing a place from which to speak. Within the language of dispersal there is a need, according to Stuart Hall, for 'arbitrary closures', points at which the infinite flux of differences is brought to a halt temporarily as a condition of speech. This moment of stasis is 'a kind of stake, a kind of wager. It says, "I need to say something, something . . . just now."' Hall sees these 'arbitrary closures' which are 'not the end' as necessary fictions which make both identity and politics possible (Hall 1987: 44).

Paul Gilroy has recently invited us to substitute 'placeless imaginings of identity' for the traditionally powerful claims of 'soil, roots and territory' and to think about movement as an alternative to the 'sedentary poetics of either blood or soil' (Gilroy 2000: 111). For Gilroy the modern African diaspora becomes a model for a new way of thinking about identity and identification, wrested away from the imperatives both of the nation and genealogy. Instead of seeing simply the trauma of an enforced separation and the exile's deracination and mourning for a lost homeland, we should use the concept of diaspora, according to Gilroy, to reorientate theories of identity 'toward contingency, indeterminacy, and conflict' (p.128). Instead of the idea of a journey towards 'the destination that a completed identity might represent', Gilroy, not unlike Hall, suggests more contingent and temporary linkages, shifting webs or networks which allows us to perceive 'new understandings of self, sameness and solidarity'. Such linkages transform notions of both space and identity and create 'new possibilities and new pleasures': 'Invariably promiscuous diaspora and the politics of commemoration it specifies challenge us to apprehend mutable forms that can redefine the idea of culture through a reconciliation with movement and complex, dynamic variation' (pp.129–30).

'Commemoration' in this context does not refer to some unchanging core of memory but to the continual act of reprocessing and modifying it in the present. This is important when we consider the autobiographical writing of two postcolonial writers, V.S. Naipaul and Michael Ondaatje, both of whom have offered problematic accounts of their 'origins' in terms of shifting and unstable memories, fragments of discourse and stories which are not anchored in 'fact'. Ondaatje's 'return' journeys to Sri Lanka in *Running in the Family* (1984) allow him access only to 'long lists of confused genealogies and rumour' (Ondaatje 1984: 205) while Naipaul's 'Prologue to an Autobiography' (1984) must deal with a family history of migration from India to Trinidad, now lost in oblivion: 'I knew only what I knew or was told. Beyond (and sometimes within) people's memories was undated time, historical darkness (Naipaul 1984: 51).

Significantly, both of these works are also travel books which put the author's 'I' into movement, not allowing any setttled perspective, and reconsidering 'home' through the eyes of a stranger. Ondaatje returning to Sri Lanka is both the 'foreigner' and 'the prodigal who hates the foreigner' as alienation and nostalgia constantly displace each other (Ondaatje 1984: 79).The book opens with an italicized passage, written, as if by a stranger, in the third person, which situates the writer in the landscape he has returned to, familiar to him from childhood, but also strangely transformed by his night-mare into a barren place which leaches sustenance from his body. Sri Lanka, so the next section tells us, has enticed him back through a dream – 'what began it all was the bright bone of a dream' (p.21) – but the dream, like the nightmare, also suggests a breaking down of boundaries and the disorientation of the subject. The starkly contrasting geographies of Toronto, where he now lives, with its 'brittle air' and snowy 'almost impassable' streets and the tropical landscape of Sri Lanka, become strangely merged in his mind as he recalls the 'frozen opera' of his family (pp.22–3). The problem becomes one of how to locate the subject across countries when there is no possible linear narrative of return, no clear place of origin. Ondaatje's search for his ancestry is constantly frustrated by a complex history of migration and the chaotic telling of family stories which never allow him to get things 'straight' (p.105). Even the name 'Ondaatje' is 'a new name' formed from a parody of Dutch, deflected from the 'original' by its iteration in different languages. Neither do the historical records afford any 'clarity', but either offer faded ruins or a proliferating jumble of names: 'We had not expected to find more than one Ondaatje here but the stones and pages are full of them' (p.66).

The title *Running in the Family* suggests the mobility of the subject who must travel across spatial and historical differences, assembling a narrative and a self from fragments of 'rumour', gossip and observation. It also, however, refers to the shared family traits that provide a connection, though the irony is that these – drinking and telling stories – are precisely the characteristcs that destabilize a relation to 'truth', producing fantasy and excess. Ondaatje is carried away on the 'wave' of his party at the beginning of the book, just as he is by the story of his grandmother, and just as she is, after a drinking bout, by the mythic flood (Ondaatje 1984: 23). 'Once a friend had told me that it was only when I was drunk that I seemed to know exactly what I wanted', Ondaatje tells us (p.22). Drunkenness paradoxically bestows certainty, but on a subject who has already become destabilized or Other: 'Dancing, balancing a wine glass on my forehead and falling to the floor . . . I knew I was already running' (ibid.).

Naipaul's 'Prologue to an Autobiography' deals not with an actual but an imaginative return to the childhood memories which prompted his own first attempts to write a story. Significantly it is the memory of a 'traveller', Bogart, and, in particular, a voice from the street in Port of Spain calling his name, which inspires his first writing and thus initiates him into his identity as a writer. The character, as it turns out, calls up for Naipaul a complicated history of migration which partly overlaps with his own family history:

> So there was a migration from India to be considered, a migra-
> tion within the British Empire. There was my Hindu family, with
> its fading memories of India; there was India itself. And there
> was Trinidad, with its past of slavery, its mixed population, its
> racial antagonisms and its changing political life; once part of
> Venezuela and the Spanish Empire, now English-speaking.
>
> (Naipaul 1984: 27)

For Naipaul it is at first difficult to think of writing outside a European context: he thinks of himself as coming from 'an intellectually restricted world', deprived of the 'background of knowledge' which is available for the English or French writer (Naipaul 1984: 27). In order to become a writer he has had to come to England. However, not only does his writing come from memories of displacement, he writes in the 'freelances' room' at the BBC, without the status of being 'staff', among the movement, anxieties and chat of his colleagues (p.22). In other words, he has discovered an alternative scene of writing, another way of locating the writer as participating in movement, rather than drawing on a settled community, and as a consequence found his own subject.

This is the reason why Naipaul juxtaposes his 'Prologue to an Autobiography' with a travel sketch 'The Crocodiles of Yamoussoukro' and sees them both as about 'the process of writing' (Naipaul 1984: 9). Travel undermines the possibility of locatedness, producing temporary points of stasis or stations of observation for the writing subject. Of Naipaul's African destination in the Ivory Coast, Yamoussoukro, a friend says: 'Try to get there at night. You'll see the double row of lights. You'll wonder where you are. And in the morning you'll see that you are nowhere' (p.82). It is that double sense of being somewhere and nowhere that Naipaul pursues as a writer and finds reproduced in the diasporic community he encounters. The difference between people – 'there were expatriaties and expatriates' (p.157) – is less where they come from, or some kind of identity forged through race, than what they can make of where they are. For Arlette, a West Indian woman who has married an Ivorian man and been abandoned by him, 'To live in Africa . . . was to have all one's ideas and values questioned. And it was good, she added, for that to happen' (p.106).

Paul Gilroy draws attention to the way ideas of nation have drawn on notions of strict gender hierarchy in order to ensure 'the continuance of blood lines': 'The integrity of the nation becomes the integrity of its masculinity. Indeed it can only be a nation if the correct version of gender hierarchy has been established and reproduced' (Gilroy 2000: 127). Diaspora, he suggests, could allow us to valorize forms of kinship other than national and familial ones. In both the texts that I have been looking at, the autobiographical subjects attempt to rediscover a relationship to a father who has been largely absent from their childhood, only to find that the father is other than they thought he was. Naipaul's belief in his father as literary mentor and 'reformer' is undermined by the discovery of his part in a traditional Hindu sacrifice and subsequent madness: 'The house where this terror befell him became unendurable to him. He left it. He became a wanderer' (Naipaul 1984: 71). Ondaatje's father is also a 'runaway', unfixable as the 'real Mervyn' (Ondaatje 1984: 175), the subject of stories which Ondaatje 'cannot come to terms with' (p.181). The role of the father in both these texts is problematic, disorientating, unable to secure the son's identity; instead the sons must strive for an affinity which has nothing to do with the handing on of power.

It is appropriate that in this chapter, which began with issues of gender, we should also return to them at the end and that it is now the father's role, rather than the mother's, that is being questioned. The autobiographical subject is cast adrift from patriarchal origins and must endlessly reinvent themselves, their location and community along with new forms of autobiography. Anxiety, as Gilroy suggests, may result, but also perhaps insight and pleasure (Gilroy 2000: 129). With Naipaul's Arlette we might want to say that though everything has become unstable, 'it was good . . . for that to happen' (Naipaul 1984: 106).

4

PRACTISING AUTOBIOGRAPHY

PERSONAL CRITICISM

This final chapter will return to an issue raised briefly in the Introduction, namely the interrelationship of criticism and auto-biography. So far we have mostly surveyed either autobiographical texts or theoretical and critical texts *about* autobiography. The exceptions have been texts by Barthes and Derrida which have interrogated the boundary between different kinds of discourse and used the autobiographical, albeit in an attenuated or fragmented form, as a source of pleasure and critique. Not surprisingly, therefore, it is poststructuralism that has seemed to provide the intellectual atmosphere in which claims to critical objectivity have been questioned over the past fifteen years and that has opened to debate the function, or indeed the necessity, of the personal or autobiographical *within* criticism.

For some this question, being broached belatedly in the 1990s under the banner of 'personal criticism', is scarcely a new one. In 1996 in a 'Forum' on the 'place, nature or limits of the personal' in criticism, published by the Modern Language Association, Jane Gallop 'snidely' suggested that far from being a 'new phenomenon', the personal within criticism was a commonplace and that scholarship had always been 'replete with personal narratives'. For Gallop it was more a case of where and how one looked: the personal was there but safely relegated to prefaces, acknowledgements, dedications and footnotes. However, for Gallop, the belief on the critic's part that the personal, while sufficiently important to the work to be mentioned, could be 'cordoned off' or pushed to the margins of the text, failed to take account of how it would also leave traces in the text, in moments of rhetorical intensity, for instance, or oddly resonant words and examples. Personal affect, according to Gallop, was always trying to get itself written, deforming both the smoothness and clarity of critical discourse (Forum 1996: 1149–50). Other contributors to the Forum agreed. Poststructuralism had not so much released a new form of writing as precipitated the recognition of what is, in effect, an inevitability. All that was new, according to Norman Holland, was a different attitude of acceptance and enjoyment: 'We are, willy-nilly, personal', he wrote. 'Let's go with it, then. Let's enjoy it. Let's chuck the pretensions to infallibility customary to our profession and have some fun' (p.1147). For others the 'personal' offered a different pedagogical model, an opportunity to acknowledge the limits of one's knowledge and understanding, to engage theoretical issues without necessarily employing a language which will alienate most readers (p.1153). It suggested that the critic is not contributing, as George T. Wright contends, 'another stolid block in the great pyramid of objective knowledge' but offering a 'probably flawed contribution' to a continuing dialogue with other scholars (p.1159). Personal criticism suggested, therefore, a more localized setting for critical writing and more modest ambitions.

However, as Claudia Tate pointed out in her contribution to this same debate, the recognition that 'scholarly prose, like imaginative literature, is inevitably personal' also derives from serious political concerns (Forum 1996: 1147). What is at stake is who speaks or rather who is authorized to speak. An objective critical stance which 'claims to speak for everyone' has, according to Tate, been exclusive and has disenfranchised alternative points of view. Such 'masterly' discourses, which critics either mimicked or were silenced by, masked an ideological investment in 'white patriarchal law'. A 'multitude of personal expressions' is both more democratic and representative of the plurality of 'personal and cultural narratives' that, in fact, determine the identity of critics (p.1148). Indeed many of the contributors to this debate who are advocates of the personal within criticism speak from 'minority' positions, as gay, immigrant, black, Asian or female, and see the personal as both a risk and an opportunity: a risk because for the 'minority' writer, as Joonok Huh argues, there is no already assured public role which will make the 'personal' safe, transforming it into another form of public performance; an opportunity because it is a way of getting free from 'established paradigms and norms' and 'seizing the initiative of utterance' (pp.1156–7).

This critical Forum rehearses many of the arguments we have already encountered in relation to autobiography, most notably in the recognition of how a universal or objective point of view implies a particular ideology of the subject. However, our exploration of autobiography also suggested a need to be sceptical about the claim that the personal can ever automatically guarantee authenticity; often, as we have seen, the subject is simply exchanging one discursive position for another, and there are perils in any claim to 'identity' which perceives the subject as unitary, and restricts its perspectives, its movement or collaboration in other discourses. 'I' can also raise problems about privilege and exclusion, and create anxieties not only about who is speaking and who by implication is not, but also about where 'I' am speaking from and for whom. These anxieties, of necessity, carry across into personal criticism.

The term 'personal criticism', whatever its wider historical relevance as an idea, was coined in the 1990s and has been associated in particular with two books published within a year of each other: Mary Ann Caws' *Women of Bloomsbury* (1990) and Nancy K. Miller's *Getting Personal* (1991); however these books also have slightly different approaches and rationales. Mary Ann Caws returned to the moment of writing *Women of Bloomsbury* from a later perspective in the 'Forum' and expressed her dissatisfaction with two aspects of her book: the first was the 'personal-pronoun problem' and the patterns of inclusion and exclusion it cannot help but create; the second was the 'tentativeness' and 'passivity' of her writing (Forum 1996: 1160). In 1990, 'personal criticism' had been her attempt to lend intimacy and warmth to her criticism both as a move away from 'impersonality' and a way of getting closer to, or even 'mingling' with, the lives of the women she was writing about (Caws 1990: 2). In retrospect she felt her writing to be too merged with her subject, not forceful enough: 'I wanted to be both passionate and compassionate but I could not express my wanting in a form hard enough' (Forum 1996: 1161). One might perhaps say that there are not in fact two issues here but one, and that the problem with personal pronouns has returned, transposed into a particular writing style. In this idealized form of critical intimacy, with its belief in 'involvement and in coherence, in warmth and in relation', there is little room for difference and no understanding of the political stakes or locatedness of the subject (Caws 1990: 3). Comprehending the relationship between identity and difference, sameness and otherness, requires, as we have seen, a critical and reflective vocabulary which is rooted in political understanding. Is the personal ever enough? Is it, indeed, only or ever really, personal?

Nancy K. Miller's book *Getting Personal* emerged from her long involvement with feminist criticism; as such it is not 'anti-theory' but rather another turn within theory, a deliberate 'turning theory back on itself' (Miller 1991: 5). Miller offers a complex analysis of personal criticism as arising out of a particular nexus of critical concerns. First, she points to a dissatisfaction with the 'absent' subject of theory whose authority rested on not owning its own necessary locatedness as a social subject: the fact that it is white, male, heterosexual, or as in the case of Paul de Man, affiliated with fascism. This dissatisfaction she sees as giving rise to 'identity politics' and a wide range of different social groupings which, however, cannot avoid equally contentious claims to representativity, the problem of speaking *as* or speaking *for* that continually returns and which seems impossible to resolve in any final way (Miller 1991: 20).

For Miller this relation of the subject to theory has a particular gender inflection. While men have tended to stake their critical authority on an 'overweighted' relation to theory and to disregard their relation to the personal, feminism has 'interrogated' how knowledge is produced and has developed an understanding of the personal as itself theoretical (Miller 1991: 21). The point, therefore, is not to offer the personal and the theoretical as contrasting and mutually exclusive modes but to see their implication in each other. For Miller personal criticism becomes a way of exposing the basis of critical and theoretical writing; it stages the critic's own relation to the ideas:

> By turning its authorial voice into spectacle, personal writing theorizes the stakes of its own performance: a personal materialism. Personal writing opens an inquiry on the cost of writing – critical writing or Theory – and its effects.
>
> (Miller 1991: 24)

The inclusion of the word 'performance' is important since it suggests a form of contingent positioning rather than any claim to authenticity. Miller is proposing the deliberate foregrounding of the critic within the text not in order to pre-empt theory but to speak personally within it and about it and thus also to reveal critical impersonality as just another personal stance in disguise. Miller herself indicates the dangers: a privileged few who can create interest in themselves because of the status they already have adopting a cosy self-referential style (Miller 1991: 25). At its best, as Miller both contends and has extensively demonstrated, these 'autobiographical acts' within criticism are 'enlivening' and challenging and extend, just as feminism has, the range of cultural material that is available (p. 21). However, as just another 'institutionalized' form of criticism, the risks of personal criticism could be minimal, and, at worst, mean little more than the substitution of one style of academic authority for another.

TESTIMONIES

Miller uses the 'old-fashioned' word 'engaged' for the form of criticism she is envisaging, and proposes a writing where the stakes are high enough to 'matter to others' (Miller 1991: 24). It is with a discussion of autobiography as a form of witnessing which 'matters to others' that I want now to conclude this book. Shoshana Felman's book *What Does a Woman Want?: Reading and Sexual Difference* (1993) will provide us with a connection or bridge between the topics of personal criticism and testimonial writing as well as raising crucial questions about the relation of autobiography to history. Situating her own writing in relation to personal criticism, Felman asks the difficult question of how we know that the 'personal' voice that the critic is speaking in is her own. 'Getting personal', here picking up Miller's title and critical argument, does not, according to Felman, 'guarantee that the story we narrate is wholly ours or that it is narrated in our own voice' (Felman 1993: 14). Felman is far from denying the importance of autobiography or that reading and writing has a relation to our lives that 'matters'. The problem is rather *where* autobiography is situated if, as Felman believes, our story cannot be 'self-present' to us, cannot be under the conscious control of the subject.

Felman's argument is framed as a feminist argument and as pertaining particularly to women's lives and writing. It is, as Felman argues, because women have been trained to see themselves as objects and have been positioned as Other that 'none of us, as women, has as yet, precisely, an autobiography' (Felman 1993: 14). What she proposes is autobiography as a form of testifying, to be distinguished from confession, which involves the speaker and the listener in a shared project to recover 'something the speaking subject is not – and cannot be – in possession of' (p.16). Felman points not to autobiographical moments within texts but rather to moments of resistance or hesitation between discourses – between theory and autobiography, for instance – which she sees as testifying to surprising irruptions of the Other. Whereas it may be impossible to gain direct access to ourselves, through personal criticism, for instance, it may be possible through a 'bond of reading' to access the story of the Other in these hesitations or resistances, a story which has yet to be told or understood (p.14).

At this point I want to leave the particular feminist slant of Felman's argument and turn back to her earlier work on testimony from which this later book partly derives. It is because Felman sees feminine existence as corresponding in some ways to traumatized existence that she suggests it cannot be simply remembered and narrated. According to Felman, testimony implies a relationship to events as evidence of truth without being able to provide 'a completed statement, a totalizable account of those events' (Felman 1993: 5). To testify, in its legal sense, is to produce one's speech or one's story as part of a larger verdict yet to be made. Testimony is called for in a situation where the truth is not clear, where there is already a 'crisis of truth': 'The trial both derives from and proceeds by, a crisis of evidence, which the verdict must resolve' (p.6).

For Felman testimony has become increasingly important in 'recent cultural accounts of ourselves' because it issues from and relates to the traumas of contemporary history, events like the Second World War, the Holocaust, the nuclear bomb, which overwhelm our ability to assimilate them and which exceed our capacity to understand (Felman 1993: 14). Cathy Caruth, in her important writing on trauma, has described the way traumatic memory can return unwilled, in dreams or flashbacks, for instance, but yet remain beyond the conscious recall of the subject. The traumatic history cannot become integrated into the subject's narrative or history of themselves because it was not fully experienced at the time it happened; nor is it fully comprehended when it is re-enacted in the present. In this sense it is a history that literally 'has no place' but is known only through a departure from it and in its insistent and terrifying return (Caruth 1995: 153).

Charlotte Delbo, a survivor of Auschwitz, has described just such a splitting within her 'self' between 'deep-lying memory' and 'ordinary memory':

> I live within a twofold being. The Auschwitz double doesn't bother me, doesn't interfere with my life. As though it weren't I at all. Without this split I would not have been able to revive.
>
> (Delbo 1990: 3)

Delbo's survival has depended on isolating her Auschwitz 'memories' which remain inaccessible to any narrative account of them: 'It is not from deep memory that my words come' (Delbo 1990: 3). Instead they return, unbidden, in dreams which overwhelm her sense of the present: 'It takes days for everything to get back to normal, for everything to get shoved back inside memory, and for the skin of memory to mend again' (ibid.). As Cathy Caruth notes, 'the traumatized . . . carry an impossible history within them, or they become themselves the symptom of a history that they cannot entirely possess' (Caruth 1995: 5).

For Caruth the implications of trauma are profound and raise questions about both historical representation and understanding. Trauma poses the problem of an inability to witness historical events except 'at the cost of witnessing oneself'. The experience, in a sense, can only be perceived as a gap, or an absence of any direct representation, in the 'collapse of understanding' (Caruth 1995: 7). However, the impossibility of articulating a comprehensible narrative, according to Caruth, does not negate the possibility of a 'transmissible truth' (p.154). It is precisely by refusing coherent narrative that a space can be opened up for 'a testimony that can speak beyond what is already understood' (p.155). This also requires a particular kind of listening and collaboration between the speaker and the listener. The listener also bears a responsibility to listen not only to an account of the event but the speaker's traumatic departure from it: 'The history of a trauma, in its inherent belatedness, can only take place through the listening of another' (p.11). The listener takes on, as it were, the ethical responsibility of bearing witness to what testimonial writing cannot directly represent, and breaking down the isolation imposed by the nature of the event. It is part of the argument, of course, that this traumatic history which exceeds the individual concerns us all.

George Perec's text *W or History of Childhood* is strangely assembled from two texts, which apparently have nothing in common. However, Perec warns us in an unpaginated and untitled Preface that 'they are in fact inextricably bound up with each other, as though neither could exist on its own' (Perec 1996). The one text is a non-narrative and fragmentary set of memories and meditations on Perec's wartime Jewish childhood; the other is a fictional account of the faraway island of W, which has built a society devoted to athletic prowess and competition but which is gradually transformed into a concentration camp ruled by a completely arbitrary set of laws that deny its inhabitants both agency and humanity.

Perec's autobiographical text, full of hiatuses and repetitions, is both an approach to remembering his parents and an acknowledgement of the impossibility of ever healing through words the trauma of their absence. All he can do is go on repeating in different words without hope of return. His parents' absence, at a time before he could understand what was happening, prompts the need to write now without necessarily allowing him to possess his subject or revive their presence. There is both a personal and ethical imperative to remember, not to surrender to the 'unsayable', but which must nevertheless encounter and keep encountering the blank and traumatic nullity of their absence:

> I am not writing in order to say that I shall say nothing, I am not writing to say that I have nothing to say. I write: I write because we lived together, because I was once amongst them, a shadow amonst their shadows, a body close to their bodies. I write because they left in me their indelible mark, whose trace is writing. Their memory is dead in writing; writing is the memory of their death and the assertion of my life.
>
> (Perec 1996: 42)

Perec's father died fighting in France in 1940; his mother was deported to Auschwitz in 1943. Perec gives us several different accounts of his departure, aged 6, from his mother, whom he was never to see again. The memory is briefly outlined in Section 8 when Perec remembers that, though he had no broken bones, he had his arm in a sling and that his mother bought him a comic entitled *Charlie and the Parachute*. He returns to this memory in Section 10, revising now the detail that he was wearing a sling and telling us that in fact he had a rupture and was wearing a truss. In restrospect there seems to be a common thread of imagery: 'A triple theme runs through this memory: parachute, sling, truss: it suggests suspension, support, almost artificial limbs. To be I need a prop' (Perec 1996: 55). Later, the parachute recurs in an actual experience of making a parachute jump in 1958:

> I suddenly saw, in the very instant of jumping, one way of deciphering the text of this memory: I was plunged into nothing-ness; all the threads were broken; I fell, on my own, without any

support. The parachute opened. The canopy unfurled, a fragile and firm suspense before the controlled descent.

(Ibid.)

The full meaning of the trauma of departure is only decipherable belatedly. As Eleanor Kaufman notes, it is not until after the war that real knowledge of the trauma is possible – that this was a final departure from his mother – nor till much later yet with the parachute jump and the experience of physical falling, that he can re-experience the inner trauma of plummeting without support and understand its meaning (Kaufman 1998: 45). Indeed we are never told when Perec realizes that his mother will not return; when, in effect, the trauma of her departure is understood and fully experienced. This trauma, the reality of the first trauma, is still absent from Perec's text.

The other story, the story of W, had its origins, so Perec tells us, in a childhood fantasy. Rediscovered, it stood in for the memories of his childhood which Perec long claimed not to have: 'In a way, if not the story of my childhood, then at least a story of my childhood' (Perec 1996: 6). Rewriting it in the 1960s, Perec allows it to be invaded by, or to become fused with, the historical events it was designed to conceal, or which were not fully known to the adolescent who first invented the island: 'W is no more like my Olympic fantasy than that Olympic fantasy was like my childhood'. It is precisely in the passage from one form of fantasy to the other that the memory resides, the sinister doubling or gradual revelation of what lies behind the fantasy, or is implicit in its folds: 'In the crisscross web they weave as in my reading of them I know there is to be found the inscription and the description of the path I have taken, the passage of my history and the story of my passage' (Perec 1996: 7).

It is also significant that the fiction of W begins with the story of a voyage to find the body of a child who has been shipwrecked along with his mother. The child was apparently 'deaf and dumb' for reasons that 'could only be ascribed to some infantile trauma whose precise configuration unfortunately remained obscure despite examinations by numerous psychiatrists' (Perec 1996: 23). As Nicola King notes, 'A lost and traumatised child is at the centre of the text' (King 2000: 129) whose name, we may add, is also given to the man asked to search for him. This story, while not in any way referring to a memory, yet holds the memory at its heart.

If Perec's W testifies to a traumatic history precisely through its absences, its uncertainties and its fictional rewritings, I want to conclude with a text which raises a different set of problems, which, while offering itself as a Holocaust survivor's testimony, has in fact turned out to be a fiction. Binjamin Wilkomirski's *Fragments: Memories of a Childhood 1939–1948* (1996) was offered as the recovered childhood memories of Binjamin Wilkomirski who had survived the slaughter of his parents and his own imprisonment in the death camps, and who records, convincingly, the images and fragments through which those memories surface and begin to be understood. Wilkomirski, who still apparently defends the authenticity of his account and believes in his identity as a survivor, has argued that 'it was always the free choice of the reader to read my book as literature or to take it as a personal document' (Gibbons and Moss 1999: 3). However, the shifting from one genre to another has been profoundly disturbing to readers and, as if embarrassed by their mistake, the publishers have withdrawn the book. To return to the courtroom scene which defines the meaning of testifying, Wilkomirski, it seems, has been convicted of providing false testimony.

Should it matter? We have seen how impossible it is to decide once and for all about the status of autobiography as either truth or fiction, and this text would seem to suggest that even testimony, with all its ethical weighting, is as unstable as a category as autobiography and could be subject to impersonation. In the future it may be possible to understand Wilkomirski's obsession with the Holocaust and absorption of the historical archive of trauma as telling us something, beyond individual pathology, about the pathology of history whose traumatic effects spread uncontrollably and implicate us in ways we do not as yet understand. This might also allow us to see through the fiction to history again. It is appropriate that this book should conclude with these problems of genre, truth and interpretation. While autobiography supplies few certainties or answers, its study leads us to engage with some of the most intractable and important cultural questions of our time.

GLOSSARY

absence a concern with what is missing from a literary work, rather than what is to be found there. Since the publication of Pierre Macherey's *A Theory of Literary Production* (1978) such absences have been given more attention. Macherey draws on Freud to emphasize his point that absence is necessary for identification and existence, and as a follower of Louis Althusser (the French Marxist philosopher), links absence with IDEOLOGY, due to ideologies' perceived failure to acknowledge their own condition. In literary texts absence is not always related to subject matter; it can also relate to style.

allegory a piece of literature written in such a way as to have two different frames or levels of meaning. An allegorical interpretation draws attention to meanings within literature other than those which are made explicit by the work.

alterity the state of being OTHERwise, different, diverse.

canon deriving from Christian debate around whether the Hebrew Bible should be granted divine authority. Used in literary criticism to refer to (1) texts indisputably by one author, (2) works set apart from others because of their quality. Included texts are agreed on by universities, the most unassailable position being granted to the works of Shakespeare, with the most extreme viewpoint being the refusal to call any text from outside of the canon 'literature'. In recent times alternative canons, such as a feminist canon, have been proposed, to exist alongside the accepted canon. However, those who promote the traditional canon do not acknowledge alternatives. Supporters of the canon insist that it is not inflexible, but many critics feel that canonization encourages standardized readings.

deconstruction a term associated with the work of the French philosopher Jacques Derrida, deconstructionist readings attempt to undermine Western metaphysics by revealing the workings of its logocentricism (reliance on a fixed centre or PRESENCE). It questions any claims towards a moment of pure origin, or essence, and whilst acknowledging such large theses as 'God', 'Truth', and 'The SUBJECT', always seeks to question their authority. Deconstruction attempts to negate the apparent 'logic' of binary hierarchies, and is a vital component of POSTSTRUCTURALISM. Deconstruction cannot help but borrow from the system it is questioning (use of language, for example), and in its attempts to avoid this it can seem frustratingly obscure.

difference the source of this, now widely applied, concept lies within the structural linguistics of Ferdinand de Saussure, who operated on the premise that language works as a system of differences, using signs (accepted words) to refer to objects mutually recognised as that being signified. Binary opposition is the starkest form of difference and is used to form part of structural textual analysis. An awareness of difference allows for textual readings which are sensitive to such oppositions as the dominant and the MARGINalized. Looking at texts in this way has had a huge impact on discussions of identity as it opens up multiple questions about the notion of the social and sexual self.

Difference is widely referred to in feminist criticism, in particular its inference that we are all dependent for meaning upon what we *are not*. Feminist criticism use of the term falls into three broad categories; *Sexual difference* (turning upon ESSENTIALISM), *Sites of difference* (e.g. uneven distribution of power in gender, race and class) and *Multiple differences* between people (stressing need for plurality).

Derrida's coinage of the term as *différance* combines 'differing' with 'deferral', to emphasize his point that meaning is deferred, due to being in a process of continuous construction.

discourse a term associated with the work of Michel Foucault, who connects it to the mediation of power and authority within society. It denotes a socially and historically situated use of language – a discursive practice – using a shared vocabulary, assumptions, values and interests, for example, legal discourse, medical discourse, poetic discourse, the discursive practice of teenage gangs. These generic groupings, of course, raise questions about the boundaries of a particular discourse. Linguistic studies cite discourse as language in use, as opposed to language as an abstract system.

essentialism the belief that attributes are inherent and distinctive to an object or person, and therefore define its 'true nature', for example, that certain qualities are universal to women, regardless of context. Often these traits are said to derive from biology and hence be inevitable; this belief is also called biological determinism. From Aristotle's writings to the present day, the issue of 'essence' continues to be debated. To argue that humans have a definable 'nature' relies on some proof of origins; making a God, or some other TRANSCENDENT being, or moment, an attractive (or convenient) proposition for some. Essentialist thought has been employed by some feminist critics in order to present a discernible 'female' nature, as the opposite of aggressive, power-seeking males. However, various other forms of feminist criticism, such as those employing psychoanalysis, DECONSTRUCTION and postmodernism, are more likely to discuss 'female nature' in terms of its being a socially constructed perception.

genre a specific type of artistic or cultural composition, identified by codes which the audience recognize. Examples of typical genre categories are science fiction, detective fiction, the musical, the western, soap operas and so on. There are also broader categories such as romance, pastoral, film noir, comedy, etc., and even broader: the novel, poetry, drama, film, etc. It is now increasingly common for texts to blur genre divisions.

humanism the word 'humanist' originally meant someone who studied the humanities, which were defined in the Middle Ages as Classical literature, rhetoric and poetry. Generally it is the belief that human values and experience are at the centre of knowledge but it has been used more recently, from a radical perspective, to denote bourgeois ideology which unthinkingly assumes the centrality of the middle-class, masculine subject.

ideology a body of ideas (masquerading as irrefutable) that reflects the beliefs consciously held by a nation, political system, etc. Frequently described as indoctrinated, and discussed in conjunction with Marx's theories of 'false consciousness'. Used in broader terms within the work of Louis Althusser, as the naturalized perception of self and the world, constructed as the individual enters the social order. Literary texts are embedded in the social and economic circumstances in which they are produced and consumed, something Althusser described as *imaginary* relationship to *real* conditions of existence. Likewise, it could be argued that a critic's own ideology will always prevent unbiased reading and writing, for example, a feminist critic will object to the ideologies of patriarchy, as a postcolonial critic will object to the ideologies of colonialism. Postmodern thinking would claim that as there is only 'falseness' anyway, there cannot be a 'false' consciousness, taking us full circle from accusing ideology of distorting reality, to claiming that there is no reality.

imaginary/symbolic/real terms developed by French psychoanalyst Jacques Lacan to describe the phases in the constitution of the psychic SUBJECT. The 'imaginary' order refers to the first, pre-Oedipal phase of infancy when the child's relation to reality is structured by pre-verbal images, fantasies and narcissistic desires, experienced in close association with the mother. The 'symbolic' order is the realm of language, where items become symbolized, and the Oedipal complex is resolved by the child's submission to the 'Law of the Father'. The unconscious forms, and the SUBJECT is placed on a quest for the unobtainable object (breast or bottle). The next stage is the 'real', beyond language, and representing the impossible, everything that could not be adequately shown by the imaginary and symbolic phases. French feminist theorists have used, and adapted, Lacan's work. Julia Kristeva has named the pre-verbal realm 'the semiotic', and argues that the desire and unity associated with this stage are not entirely repressed, whilst Luce Irigaray proclaims the need to reformulate much of the explanation of the phases, taking into account that babies are not all male.

intentionality/intentional meaning a fallacy, sometimes pursued in literary criticism, that a text may be defined in terms of its author's intentions.

intertextuality a term introduced by Julia Kristeva to denote a relation, conscious or unconscious, between texts within an apparently discrete text. More generally it indicates the penetration of any text by memories or echoes of previous texts and therefore the way all texts comprise an interaction between texts.

liberalism a term often used in conjunction with HUMANISM to denote the belief in the individual as an autonomous being which assumes its neutrality but which has been critiqued by feminists as intimately allied with patriarchal ideology.

logos a Greek word combining several meanings; that of 'the Law', 'the Word', 'sense,' and 'meaning'. A term much used by Jacques Derrida to describe schools of thought which focus on a single, controlling centre as logocentric (see DECONSTRUCTION). Derrida points out that these inward rational principles, be they applied to texts, human beings or the natural universe, cause the centre to be paradoxically both inside and outside of the 'system', as they are present, yet as an influence, prior – so absent. Such anomalies, he feels, demonstrate the illusory nature of placing our faith in inward-looking, rational principles.

margin(ality) terms used to refer to a place for repressed textual meanings, but also the position of individuals and groups who do not conform to normative assumptions, and are therefore subjected to oppression from the power structures of mainstream society. To be within the margins can be viewed as a negative and preclusive experience, or alternatively as an advantageous position, from which to comment on the larger society. The critical theories of psychoanalysis, IDEOLOGY and DECONSTRUCTION have all encouraged readers to grant validity to marginal, subordinated meanings. The spatial metaphor of centre and peripheries also owes something to the schools of thought studying cultural geography and postcolonialism. Authors too are described as occupying a marginal position, due to their social or national identity. Many authors within the school of MODERNISM were caught in the margins between cultures, and in more recent times many feminist writers have chosen to focus on the way in which patriarchal cultures allow male experience to dominate, hence marginalizing female experience.

Modernism usually refers to the artistic and cultural production, practices and attitudes arising between approximately 1890 to 1930 (exact dates are contested). The period in question correlates with the explosion of mass popular culture. Modernists proclaimed that the experimental nature of their work overhauled traditional forms, values and perceptions. Paradoxically, much modernist writing displays not only the determination to break away from the past, but also a profound suspicion of the future, with its rapid technological developments and ever-increasing commercialism. Modernist texts incorporate estrangement, montage, collage, demotic language, interior monologue, parody, pastiche and a heightened self-consciousness about the physical act of writing. Despite the work of Virginia Woolf and HD, the majority of Modernism's famous proponents were overwhelmingly male, (e.g. T.S. Eliot, James Joyce, Ezra Pound, D.H. Lawrence and Franz Kafka). Feminist criticism stresses the many women writers omitted from the modernist CANON.

New Critics the name applied to a group of American critics in the 1930s and 1940s, among whom were John Crowe Ransom, W.K.Wimsatt and Cleanth Brooks, who believed in the autonomy of literature and advocated the close reading of texts. They defined various erroneous ways of reading literature including the INTENTIONAL fallacy. The English critic F.R. Leavis was influenced by the New Criticism, though he tended to stress more than the literature role in moral and cultural education.

other a person, group or institution is placed outside the parameters of normality by being classed as 'other', and subsequently inferior, to oneself; it is therefore a process of categorization by exclusion. When used cynically, such terminology legitimates inhuman treatment, and exploitation, of 'others', on grounds of their race, gender, sexuality or appearance – which is typically described in stereotypical terms. With a capital letter the 'Other' invokes the theory of Jacques Lacan, in which the SUBJECT defines itself by comparison with some Other, and the discourse of the unconscious becomes the discourse of this Other. This idea, of the other as a part of oneself, is often used in Gothic fiction, where a monstrous double must be resisted.

performative uses theatre studies, along with the general theatricality of performance, to emphasize that identity is a social construct.

phallocentricism used in the psychoanalytic theories of Sigmund Freud and Jacques Lacan, where the phallus is cited as being central to psychological development, and the establishment of sexual difference. More broadly, the term is used of any theory, textual representation, DISCOURSE or social system which endorses the privileged symbolic power of the male over the female, thus reinforcing the inequalities of patriarchy.

The term has been much used by French feminists who associate it with logocentricism.

poststructuralism   a school of criticism that claims the text is never fixed and irrefutable, but always capable of revealing more. Its close links with DECONSTRUCTION mean that sometimes the two terms are used interchangeably. In common with the other movements with the prefix 'post' (postcolonialism, postmodernism, etc.) poststructuralism indicates both continuation, and an ongoing critique of earlier ideas, believing that meaning is not centred within a closed system, and therefore demands continuous analysis. Jacques Derrida and Roland Barthes are perhaps the two most obvious examples of components of this school, with Jacques Lacan, Louis Althusser and Michel Foucault also having affiliations, but of a more ambiguous nature.

presence   a vital element of logocentricism, in that the names relating to the principles and fundamentals, believed by some to exist at the centre of meaning, have always been designated an irrefutable presence (such as God, existence, SUBJECT, consciousness, etc.). Such words have come to represent points of authority, and hence the potential to escape from Derrida's play of DIFFERENCE.

prosopopoeia   to represent an absent or IMAGINARY person as speaking and/or acting through a rhetorical figure, or an inanimate object as embodying personal qualities (personification).

real   see imaginary.

Romanticism   a literary movement which can be dated from about 1789 to 1830. Many of its ideological assumptions can be seen as persisting to the present, in particular its central belief in the essential unity of both art and the self, and their capacity to transcend society.

subject   term for self, individual, human being, widely adopted by poststructuralist critics due to the sense of doubling it gives, in the binary opposition of subject/object. This implication of a split identity is a concept explored by psychoanalytic, feminist and cultural critics, usually encompassing readings of Sigmund Freud and/or Karl Marx.

subjectivity   the internal experience of being a SUBJECT.

symbolic   see imaginary.

transcendent   traditionally a term meaning existing beyond the created world, and therefore free from its limitations; however, Jacques Derrida's use of the word to represent a negative authoritative unity has undoubted implications for its use in literary criticism. As an example, the valorizing of white, middle-class, European males could be labelled a transcendental falsity.

unitary   the belief that words, knowledge and representations can be defined, and therefore stabilized, in a single distinct meaning, perceived as the authorized version. DECONSTRUCTIONist work on language, and psychoanalytic theories of the unconscious, directly oppose this belief, and claim language to be ambiguous, and therefore inevitably offering multiple meanings.

BIBLIOGRAPHY

Anderson, Linda (1997) *Women and Autobiography in the Twentieth Century: Remembered Futures*, Hemel Hempstead, Prentice Hall/Harvester Wheatsheaf.

Augustine, Saint (1961) *Confessions*, trans.R.S.Pine-Coffin, Harmondsworth, Penguin.

Barthes, Roland (1968) 'The Death of the Author', in Philip Rice and Patricia Waugh (eds), *Modern Literary Theory: A Reader*, London, Edward Arnold, 1989.

—— (1977) *Roland Barthes by Roland Barthes*, trans. Richard Howard, London, Macmillan. Originally published 1975.

—— (1984) *Camera Lucida*, trans. Richard Howard, London, Flamingo. Originally published 1980.

Bell, Alan (ed.) (1977) *Sir Leslie Stephen's Mausoleum Book*, Oxford, Clarendon Press.

Bell, Robert (1977) 'Metamorphosis of a Spiritual Autobiography', *ELH*: 108–126.

Benstock, Shari (1988) *The Private Self: Theory and Practice of Women's Autobiographical Writings*, London, Routledge.

Bhabha, Homi (1986) 'Signs Taken for Wonders: Questions of Ambivalence and Authority under a Tree Outside Delhi: 1817', in Henry Louis Gates Jr. (ed.) *'Race' Writing and Difference*, Chicago, IL, University of Chicago Press.

Bowie, Malcolm (1991) *Lacan*, London, Fontana Press.

Boswell, James (1950) *London Journal 1762–1763*, ed. Frederick A. Pottle, London, Heinemann.

—— (1951) *Boswell's Column*, London, William Kimber & Co.

—— (1970) *Life of Johnson*, ed. R.W.Chapman, Oxford, Oxford University Press. Originally published 1791.

Briggs, Julia (1995) 'Virginia Woolf and The Proper Writing of Lives', in John Batchelor (ed.), *The Art of Literary Biography*, Oxford, Oxford University Press.

Brodski, Bella and Schenk, Celeste (eds) (1988) *Life/Lines: Theorizing Women's Autobiography*, Ithaca, NY, Cornell University Press.

Broughton, Trev Lynn (1999) *Men of Letters, Writing Lives: Masculinity and Literary Auto/Biography in the Late Victorian Period*, London, Routledge.

Broughton, Trev Lynn and Anderson, Linda (1997) *Women's Lives/Women's Times: New Essays on Auto/Biography*, Albany, State University of New York Press.

Brown, Peter (1967) *Augustine of Hippo: A Biography*, London, Faber and Faber.

Bunyan, John (1962) *Grace Abounding to the Chief of Sinners*, ed. Roger Sharrock, Oxford, Oxford University Press. Originally published 1666.

Burke, Sean (1992) *The Death and Return of the Author*, Edinburgh, Edinburgh University Press.

Butterfield, Stephen (1974) *Black Autobiography in America*, Amherst, Amherst University Press.

Carlton, Peter J. (1984) 'Bunyan: Language, Convention, Authority', *ELH*, 51: 17–32.

Caruth, Cathy (1995) *Trauma: Explorations in Memory*, Baltimore, Johns Hopkins University Press.

Caws, Mary Ann (1990) *Women of Bloomsbury*, London, Routledge.

Chase, Cynthia (ed.) (1993) *Romanticism*, London, Longman.

Cheah, Pheng and Grosz, Elizabeth (1998) 'Of Being-Two', *Diacritics*, 28: 3–18.

Corbett, Mary Jane (1992) *Representing Femininity*, Oxford, Oxford University Press.

de Man, Paul (1979a) *Allegories of Reading: Figural Language in Rousseau, Nietzsche, Rilke and Proust*, New Haven and London, Yale University Press.

—— (1979b) 'Autobiograpy as De-Facement', *Modern Language Notes*, 94: 919–30.

—— (1993) 'Time and History in Wordsworth', in Cynthia Chase (ed.) *Romanticism*, London and New York, Longman, pp.55–77.

de Selincourt, Ernest (1932) 'Introduction', *The Prelude*, Oxford, Oxford University Press.

Delany, Paul (1969) *British Autobiography in the Seventeenth Century*, London, Routledge & Kegan Paul.

Delbo, Charlotte (1990) *Days and Memories*, trans. Rosette Lamont, Malboro, Vermont, Malboro Press.

Derrida, Jacques (1976) *Of Grammatology*, trans. Gayatri Chakravorty Spivak, Baltimore and London, Johns Hopkins University Press.

—— (1980) 'The Law of Genre', *Glyph*, 7: 202–29.

—— (1988) *The Ear of the Other: Otobiography, Transference, Translation: Texts and Discussions with Jacques Derrida*, trans. Peggy Kamuf and Avital Ronell, ed.Christie McDonald, Lincoln and London, University of Nebraska Press.

—— (1989) *Memoires: For Paul de Man*, trans, Cecile Lindsay, Jonathan

Culler, Eduardo Cadava and Peggy Kamuf, New York, Columbia University Press.

—— (1990) *Memoirs of the Blind: The Self-Portrait and Other Ruins*, Chicago, IL, University of Chicago Press.

—— (1991) 'To Speculate on Freud', in Peggy Kamuf (ed.), *A Derrida Reader: Between the Blinds*, Hemel Hempstead, Harvester Wheatsheaf.

—— (1993) 'Circumfession', in Jacques Derrida with Geoffrey Bennington, *Jacques Derrida*, Chicago, IL, University of Chicago Press.

Dollimore, Jonathan (1991) *Sexual Dissidence: Augustine to Wilde, Freud to Foucault*, Oxford, Oxford University Press.

Elam, Diane (1994) *Feminism and Deconstruction: Ms en Abyme*, London and New York, Routledge.

Feder, Ellen, Rawlinson Mary C. and Zakin, Emily (1997) *Derrida and Feminism: Recasting the Question of Woman*, London, Routledge.

Felman, Shoshana (1993) *What Does a Woman Want?: Reading and Sexual Difference*, Baltimore and London, The Johns Hopkins University Press.

Felman, Shoshana and Laub, Dori (1992) *Testimony*, London and New York, Routledge.

Fleishman, Avrom (1983) *Figures of Autobiography: The Language of Self-Writing in Victorian and Modern England*, Berkeley, Los Angeles and London, University of California Press.

Forum (1996) *PMLA*, 111: 1146–69.

Fowler, Alastair (1982) *Kinds of Literature: An Introduction to the Theory of Genres and Modes*, Oxford, Clarendon Press.

Freud, Sigmund (1935) *An Autobiographical Study*, London, The Hogarth Press.

—— (1974) 'Fraulein Elizabeth von R', in Sigmund Freud and Joseph Breuer, *Studies in Hysteria*, The Pelican Freud Library, 3, Harmondsworth, Penguin. Originally published 1893.

—— (1977) 'Dora', The Pelican Freud Library 8, Harmondsworth, Penguin. Originally published 1905.

—— (1979a) 'The Wolf Man', The Pelican Freud Library 9, Harmondsworth, Penguin. Originally published 1918.

—— (1979b) 'The Future Prospects of Psycho-analysis', The Pelican Freud Library 15, Harmondsworth, Penguin. Originally Published 1910.

Gagnier, Regenia (1991) *Subjectivities: A History of Self-Representation in Britain*, Oxford, Oxford University Press.

Gibbons, Fiachra and Moss, Stephen (1999) 'Fragments of a Fraud', *Guardian*, 15 October, pp. 2–3.

Gilroy, Paul (1993) *The Black Atlantic: Modernity and Double Consciousness*, London, Verso.

—— (2000) *Between Camps: Race Identity and Nationalism at the End of the Colour Line*, Harmondsworth, Penguin.

Graham, Elspeth, Hinds, Hilary, Hobby, Elaine and Wilcox, Helen (eds) (1989) *Her Own Life: Autobiographical Writings by Seventeenth-Century Englishwomen*, London, Routledge.

Gusdorf, Georg (1956) 'Conditions and Limits of Autobiography', reprinted in James Olney (ed.) *Autobiography: Essays Theoretical and Critical*, Princeton, NJ, Princeton University Press, 1980.

Hall, Stuart (1987) 'Minimal Selves', in *The Real Me: Postmodernism and the Question of Identity*, London, Institute of Contemporary Arts.

—— (1990) 'Cultural Identity and Diaspora', in Jonathan Rutherford (ed.), *Identity, Community, Culture, Difference*, London, Lawrence & Wishart.

Harpham, Geoffrey Galt (1995) 'Ethics', in Frank Lentricchia and Thomas McLaughlin (eds), *Critical Terms for Literary Study* Chicago, IL, and London, Chicago University Press.

Haskin, Dayton (1981) 'Bunyan, Luther, and the Struggle with Belatedness in *Grace Abounding*', *University of Toronto Quarterly*, 50: 300–13.

Hawkins, Anne (1980) 'The Double-Conversion in Bunyan's *Grace Abounding*', *Philological Quarterly*, 61: 259–76.

Hill, Christopher (1986) 'The Protestant Nation', in *The Collected Essays*, II, Amherst, The University of Massachusetts Press.

hooks, bell (1992) *Black Looks: Race and Representation*, London, Turnaround Press.

Hurston, Zora Neale (1984) *Dust Tracks on the Road*, Urbana and Chicago, University of Illinois Press. Originally published 1942.

Hyde, Mary (1977) *The Thrales of Streatham Park*, Cambridge, MA, Harvard University Press.

Jacobus, Mary (1986) *Reading Women: Essays in Feminist Criticism*, New York, Columbia University Press.

—— (1989) *Writing and Sexual Difference: Essays on The Prelude*, Oxford, Clarendon Press.

Jameson, Frederic (1981) *The Political Unconscious: Narrative as a Socially Symbolic Act*, London, Methuen.

Jay, Paul (1984) *Being in the Text: Self Representation from Wordsworth to Roland Barthes*, Ithaca, NY, Cornell University Press.

Jelinek, Estelle (1980) *Women's Autobiography: Essays in Criticism*, Bloomington and London, Indiana University Press.

Johnson, Barbara (1986) 'Thresholds of Difference: Structures of Address in Zora Neale Hurston', in Henry Louis Gates Jr. (ed.), *'Race', Writing and Difference*, Chicago, IL, University of Chicago Press.

—— (1987) 'My Monster/My Self', in *A World of Difference*, Baltimore and London, Johns Hopkins University Press.

—— (1994) *The Wake of Deconstruction*, Oxford, Blackwell.

Jouve, Nicole Ward (1991) *White Woman Speaks With Forked Tongue: Criticism as Autobiography*, New York and London, Routledge.

Kaufman, Eleanor (1998) 'Falling from the Sky: Trauma in Perec's *W* and Caruth's *Unclaimed Experience*', *Diacritics*, 28: 44–53.

King, Nicola (2000) *Narrative, Identity, Memory: Remembering the Self*, Edinburgh, Edinburgh University Press.

Kristeva, Julia (1986) 'A Question of Subjectivity – an Interview', in Philip Rice and Patricia Waugh (eds), *Modern Literary Theory: A Reader*, London, Edward Arnold, 1989.

—— (1989) *Black Sun: Melancholia and Depression*, New York, Columbia University Press.

Lacan, Jacques (1979) *The Four Fundamental Concepts of Psycho-Analysis*, Harmondsworth, Penguin.

Lang, Candace (1982) 'Autobiography in the Aftermath of Romanticism', *Diacritics*, 12: 2–16.

Lejeune, Philippe (1982) 'The Autobiographical Contract', in Tzvetan Todorov (ed.), *French Literary Theory Today* Cambridge, Cambridge University Press.

Loomba, Ania (1998) *Colonialism/Postcolonialism*, London, Routledge.

Mandel, Barett (1980) 'Full of Life Now', in James Olney (ed.), *Autobiography: Essays Theoretical and Critical*, Princeton, NJ, Princeton University Press, 1982.

Marcus, Laura (1994) *Auto/biographical Discourses*, Manchester, Manchester University Press.

Mellor, Anne (1993) *Romanticism and Gender*, New York, Routledge.

Miller, Nancy K. (1988) *Subject to Change: Reading Feminist Writing*, New York, Columbia University Press.

—— (1991) *Getting Personal*, New York and London, Routledge.

—— (1994) 'Representing Others: Gender and the Subject of Autobiography', *Differences*, 6: 1–27.

Miller, Perry (1939) *The New England Mind*, New York, Macmillan.

Misch, George (1907) *A History of Autobiography in Antiquity*, trans. E.W. Dickes, 2 vols. London, Routledge & Kegan Paul, 1950.

Mitchell, W.J.T. (1990) 'Influence, Autobiography and Literary History:

Rousseau's *Confessions* and Wordsworth's *The Prelude*', *ELH*, 57: 643–64.

Moi, Toril (1985) *Sexual/Textual Politics*, London, Methuen.

Naipaul,V.S. (1984) *Finding the Centre*, Harmondsworth, Penguin.

Nussbaum, Felicity A.(1989) *The Autobiographical Subject: Gender and Ideology in Eighteenth-Century England*, Baltimore, MD, and London, Johns Hopkins University Press.

Olney, James (1972) *Metaphors of Self: The Meaning of Autobiography*, Princeton, NJ, Princeton University Press.

—— (ed.) (1980) *Autobiography: Essays Theoretical and Critical*, Princeton, NJ, Princeton University Press.

Ondaatje, Michael (1984) *Running in the Family*, London, Picador.

Pascal, Roy (1960) *Design and Truth in Autobiography*, Cambridge, MA, Harvard University Press.

Perec, George (1996) *W or History of Childhood*, trans. David Bellos, London, The Harvell Press. Originally published 1975.

Probyn, Elspeth (1993) *Sexing the Self: Gendered Positions in Cultural Studies*, London and New York, Routledge.

Rousseau, Jean Jacques (1953) *The Confessions of Jean-Jacques Rousseau*, trans. with an introduction by J.M.Cohen, Harmondsworth, Penguin.

Rylance, Rick (1994) *Roland Barthes*, Hemel Hempstead, Harvester Wheatsheaf.

Sheringham, Michael (1993) *French Autobiography: Devices and Desires*, Oxford, Clarendon Press.

Siskin, Clifford (1988) *The Historicity of Romantic Discourse*, New York, Oxford University Press.

Smith, Robert (1995) *Derrida and Autobiography*, Cambridge, Cambridge University Press.

Smith, Sidonie (1993) *Subjectivity, Identity and the Body: Women's Autobiographical Practices in the Twentieth Century*, Bloomington, Indiana University Press.

Smith, Sidonie and Watson, Julia (eds) (1992) *De/Colonizing the Subject: The Politics of Gender in Women's Autobiography*, Minneapolis, University of Minnesota Press.

Smith, Valerie (1989) 'Black Feminist Theory and the Representation of the Other', in Robyn R.Warhol and Diane Price Lerndl (eds) *Feminisms*, London, Macmillan.

Spivak, Gayatri Chakravorty (1987) 'Sex and History in The Prelude (1805)', in *In Other Worlds: Essays in Cultural Politics*, New York and London, Methuen, pp.46–76.

Stanley, Liz (1992) *The Auto/biographical I: The Theory and Practice of Feminist Auto/biography*, Manchester, Manchester University Press.

Stanton, Domna (ed.) (1984) *The Female Autobiographer*, New York, New York Literary Forum.

Starobinski, Jean (1971a) *Jean-Jacques Rousseau: Transparency and Obstruction*, trans. Arthur Goldhammer, Chicago and London, University of Chicago Press.

—— (1971b) 'The Style of Autobiography', reprinted in James Olney (ed.), *Autobiography: Essays Theoretical and Critical*, Princeton, NJ, Princeton University Press, 1980.

Steedman, Carolyn (1986) *Landscape for a Good Woman*, London, Virago.

Sturrock, John (1993) *The Language of Autobiography: Studies in the First Person Singular*, Cambridge and New York, Cambridge University Press.

Swindells, Julia (1985) *Victorian Writing and Working Women*, Cambridge, Polity Press.

—— (ed.) (1995) *The Uses of Autobiography*, London, Taylor & Francis.

Thrale, Mrs Hester Lynch (1942) *Thraliana*, 2 vols, ed. Katharine C. Balderston, Oxford, Clarendon Press.

Tindall, William York (1934) *John Bunyan: Mechanic Preacher*, New York, Columbia University Press.

Walker, Alice (1984) *In Search of Our Mother's Gardens*, London, The Women's Press.

Weintraub, Karl (1978) *The Value of the Individual: Self and Circumstance in Autobiography*, Chicago, IL, and London, University of Chicago Press.

Wilkomirski, Binjamin (1996) *Fragments: Memories of a Childhood 1939–1948*, London, Picador.

Williams, Huntington (1983) *Rousseau and Romantic Autobiography*, Oxford, Oxford University Press.

Wiseman, Mary Bittner (1989) *The Ecstasies of Roland Barthes*, London, Routledge.

Woolf, Virginia (1967) *Collected Essays*, 4 vols, London, the Hogarth Press.

—— (1977) *A Room of One's Own*, London, Granada; first published by the Hogarth Press 1929.

—— (1978a) *Moments of Being*, ed. Jeanne Schulkind, London, Granada.

—— (1978b) *Orlando*, London, Granada.

—— (1979) 'The Journal of Mistress Joan Martyn', ed. Susan M. Squier and Louise Desalvo, *Twentieth Century Literature*, 25: 237–69.

—— (1983) *The Diary of Virginia Woolf*, ed. Anne Oliver Bell, 5 vols, Harmondsworth, Penguin.

Wordsworth, William (1805) *The Prelude*, ed. Ernest de Selincourt, Oxford, Oxford Unversity Press, 1932.

Wright, T.R. (1988) *Theology and Literature*, Oxford, Blackwell.

INDEX

NOTE: Page numbers in **bold** indicate major treatment of a subject; page numbers followed by *gl* indicate information is in a Glossary entry.